HEWLETT - PACKARD COMPANY
1501 PAGE MILL ROAD
PALO ALTO, CALIFORNIA 94304

DAVID PACKARD
CHAIRMAN EMERITUS

To all HP People:

I hope you'll enjoy this account of how Bill and I started the company and how it developed into a worldwide leader in technology, innovation and business enterprise. I have also described those HP values and management principles that together have become known as the "HP Way."

HP's success is due to the talents and dedication of you and your colleagues and of the people who have gone before you. Together we have built a truly remarkable company. I believe it is a company without peer and I hope, as you read the pages that follow, you will feel a deep sense of pride and satisfaction in what we have accomplished.

Sincerely,

David Packard

THE HP WAY

How Bill Hewlett and I
Built Our Company

by David Packard

Edited by
David Kirby with
Karen Lewis

HarperBusiness
A Division of HarperCollins*Publishers*

HarperCollins books may be purchased for educational, business, or sales promotional use. For information please write: Special Markets Department, HarperCollins Publishers, Inc., 10 East 53rd Street, New York, NY 10022.

FIRST EDITION

ISBN 0–88730–747–7

95 96 97 98 99 ❖/HC 10 9 8 7 6 5 4 3 2 1

This book is dedicated
to the memory of
Flora Hewlett and Lucile Packard.

Their steadfast encouragement and
their active participation in
the early years of our company
were the genesis of the HP Way.

Contents

Acknowledgments

This book was edited by Dave Kirby and Karen Lewis, who provided invaluable assistance in this role.

Many other people provided assistance to me, without which the book might never have been written. Among them, I especially wish to thank Al Bagley, Bill Terry, Dick Hackborn, Barney Oliver, Art Fong, Dick Were, and my personal secretary, Gretchen Dennis, who helped to put it all together. I'd like also to acknowledge the assistance of Margaret Paull, my secretary at the company.

The accuracy in this record is largely their contribution; the errors are fully my responsibility.

In the section about my involvement as the U.S. deputy secretary of defense, I have included only those activities that involved applying the HP Way in the DOD and some of the important management changes involving the Chairman of the Joint Chiefs.

Prologue

In the fall of 1930 I left my hometown of Pueblo, Colorado, to enroll at Stanford University. There I met another freshman, Bill Hewlett.

In those days, if a student planned a career in a technical field, science and mathematics could be included in the first two years of general studies. I had decided I wanted to be an electrical engineer, and Bill thought he might be interested in medicine or engineering, so he and I were in many of the same classes during our freshman and sophomore years. By our senior year we had become good friends.

Through a combination of circumstances that I will describe in the following pages, Bill, some friends, and I decided to start our own business when we graduated. We actually started our business in 1939, some years later.

During the first few years of operating the Hewlett-Packard Company, Bill and I developed a way of doing things, a management style, that included some features not common to management in those days. This became known as the HP Way.

This book is the story of Bill Hewlett and me and the Hewlett-Packard Company, which we spent our lives building and operating.

THE HP WAY

Chapter 1

Pueblo to Stanford

AS WE GET OLDER we have the opportunity to look back over many years and see how certain events, seemingly unimportant at the time, had a profound effect in shaping our business or professional careers.

In my own case there were two such events. One occurred in the summer of 1929 when I was given a tour of Stanford University. This introduction to Stanford led to my decision to attend the university. The second event, related to the first, was becoming acquainted with Professor Fred Terman at Stanford. It was Fred who sparked my interest in electronics and who later encouraged and helped Bill Hewlett and me go into business for ourselves. His interest and faith in our abilities, even at our young age and in the midst of the Great Depression, gave us confidence and helped set a course for us.

I was born in Pueblo, Colorado, in 1912. My father was a lawyer and my mother a high school teacher. They met at Colorado College in Colorado Springs, and after they were married they moved to Pueblo, which was my father's home. My younger sister, Ann Louise, was born in 1915.

Pueblo in 1912 resembled less a midwestern farm community than it did a western frontier city or border town. There was a steel mill and several foundries that smelted ore from Leadville and other mines in the Rocky Mountains to the west. Pueblo was tough and violent, with immigrant workers, a few gangsters, and lots of brothels and saloons. Street fights and shootings were not uncommon.

We lived on the north side of the city right next to the prairie. I could cross the street in front of our house and find horned toads (which are almost extinct today) and wild onions and cactus, which often gave shelter to rattlesnakes.

We could look across the prairie and see Pikes Peak about fifty miles to the north, and about thirty miles to the west, the Wet Mountain Range. I spent many hours roaming the prairie, sometimes with childhood friends, sometimes alone, until my high school years, when studies and school activities consumed most of my time. But in those early years of roaming, my love of nature was born.

One of my early recollections of Pueblo was the great flood of 1921. I recall going downtown with my father and seeing mud about four feet deep. Another memorable sight was a railroad boxcar stuck in the second-floor window of one of the main buildings. A fleet of four-wheel-drive army trucks was brought in to haul the mud and debris out of the city and dump it in the prairie about a mile north of our house. A number of kids from our neighborhood went out and sifted through the mud, intrigued with the possibility of finding something of value. But I don't recall finding anything useful.

Our house in Pueblo was on the corner of Twenty-ninth Street and High Street. It was set back from Twenty-ninth Street to provide for a large yard. The yard was divided into two roughly equal sections by a row of lilac bushes. In the front section was a rose arbor and a bed of peonies, with the rest in lawn. In the rear section were some fruit trees, a vegetable garden, and a pool near a wildflower garden.

My father had no interest in gardening, and so the entire garden was my mother's project. I started help-

Dave Packard with his mother, Ella, by the garden in Pueblo, Colorado, 1922.

ing my mother when I was quite young, and gardening became a lifelong interest for me. I also found it to be an excellent recreational activity, for one quickly forgets the troubles of the world when absorbed with gardening. As an adult, wherever we were located for a period of time, I had a garden, and now that I am retired, I enjoy devoting more time to gardening projects. I also have an avid interest in farming and ranching.

Early Experiments

As a very young child, I must have had some aptitude for science and math; my parents did nothing to discourage me—I spent hours curled up with the family *World Book Encyclopedia*, studying every entry on the natural sciences. I also conducted my own experiments. I remember that while quite young I got a thrill from looking at pictures of railroads, bridges, motors, generators, and other mechanical and electrical equipment. I tried to simulate some of these devices with small-scale models in our backyard. An older boy, Lloyd Penrose, lived across the alley behind us. His mother and sister had tuberculosis, and Lloyd worked in the evenings at an amusement park across town to help support them. He also helped me with my models and devices, and we became good friends. Later on, since he could not afford to go to college, Lloyd joined the navy, and we kept in touch for many years.

I also was interested in explosives. Friends and I

would make gunpowder using ammonium nitrate instead of sodium nitrate, which was used in common gunpowder. The ammonium nitrate was more active. We also made ammonium iodide by dissolving iodine crystals in ammonia. We then separated out the ammonium iodide with filter paper, and when it was dry it would explode from a mere touch.

About a mile from our house was a sand mill where blasting powder was kept in five-gallon drums. We found that a tablespoon or two of powder was often left in the empty drums, which gave us another source of explosive powder.

Playing with explosives was a dangerous pastime, as I learned from experience. Once, while I held a piece of copper tubing loaded with explosive powder in my left hand and pounded the tubing closed with a hammer in my right hand, it exploded! Lloyd was with me, and we wrapped my bleeding hand in a sheet of cloth and went to the office of a Dr. Wise to have it sewn up. He was not a very good surgeon, and I have lived with a distorted left thumb ever since. Needless to say, this ended my experiments with explosives.

Radio was another keen interest. I recall my first vacuum tube. I connected this tube with a variable condenser, a coil, a grid lead, an A battery, a B battery, and a set of headphones on our dining room table. There was great excitement as my family and I took turns listening to WHO in Des Moines, Iowa, an astonishing six hundred miles from Pueblo! I put together a fairly sophisticated vacuum-tube receiver when I was twelve

Radio 9DRV, Dave Packard's ham radio station in Pueblo, 1928.

years old. By the time I reached Centennial High School I was a proficient radio operator and became secretary of the San Isabel Radio Club. This in turn enabled me to attend the statewide ham radio conventions in Denver.

My father was not a fisherman, but I had a friend, Wendell Spear, whose family would spend two weeks every summer fishing in the Gunnison River area. They took me with them several times. Thus, my interest in trout fishing began when I was about ten years old. At that time the limit on trout was fifty fish a day. Each of us had no difficulty catching the limit. I can still remember that it was very tiresome hiking several miles back to camp with a creel full of fish. The Spears would bring along several small wooden kegs to salt the trout and preserve it for winter. Every night we would hang the fish on a line to dry and in the morning put them in a keg—a layer of fish and then a layer of salt and so on until the keg was full. When the kegs were opened in the winter, one could hardly tell the difference between the fish and the salt! It would have been much better to smoke the fish, but none of us knew how to do that. When I was in high school, several of my friends and I would go fishing for a week or two every summer, but we gave up salting our catch.

When I was eleven years old, my father bought me a pony named Laddie. He was a fairly large stallion with lots of energy. I would saddle him up in the morning, and when I got on him, he would buck and rear up. Then, when my father hit him on his behind with a broom, he would go out the driveway at a full gallop and go north on Twenty-ninth Street toward the prairie. He would spot a patch of alfalfa, race up to it at full speed, then plant his forelegs to stop and eat. I would go flying over his head and hit the ground. He knew all the tricks to get rid of his rider, such as running next to a barbed-wire fence to scrape him off. My father wouldn't let me quit, however, so I finally got so I could handle him, and we became good friends. I would often ride him out in the prairie to hunt. On one of the last rides I remember, we were going full speed when he stepped in a prairie dog hole and we both rolled in the dust. Fortunately he did not break a leg, nor did I. This was a

*Dave Packard holds
Laddie's reins for his sister,
Ann Louise, 1928.*

hard way to learn how to handle a horse, but over the years I have done a lot of riding, some of it in tough mountain country.

In the last year of grade school I began taking violin lessons. I enjoyed them to a degree but did not practice enough because other activities always seemed to have a higher priority. My father had a bachelor friend, Mr. Pope, who also played the violin. He would often join us at home on Sunday evenings, where my mother, who played the piano, and Mr. Pope and I would play for an hour or two.

During my first year in high school I played second

fiddle in the orchestra and tuba in the band. I have always enjoyed music but never spent enough time with an instrument to become a very good player.

Centennial High School

Centennial had the traditional high school academic program. Our class sponsor was Miss Melchor, the Latin teacher. I had to work very hard at Latin, but the math and science courses were easy because I already knew about as much as the teachers did. I was elected president of my class all four years.

My involvement in athletics began in my junior year, and in my senior year we had championship teams in football, basketball, and track. In the state high school basketball tournament, we lost the final game to a team from a small town in eastern Colorado called Joes. I was selected as the all-state basketball center.

In the all-state track meet I won the high jump, the broad jump (now the long jump), the low hurdles, the high hurdles, and the discus, setting a new record for the all-state meet. The great hurdler from the University of Colorado, Gordon Allott, was studying law in my father's office and gave me some excellent coaching. He later was elected to the U.S. Senate and was very encouraging to our company while serving there.

I enjoyed athletics and learned some lessons that were helpful in managing Hewlett-Packard. I remem-

ber particularly a Mr. Porter, who took a personal interest in both grade school and high school athletes in
Pueblo. He said that many times two teams playing for
a championship each have equally good players. In this
case teamwork becomes very important, especially in
the split-second plays: Given equally good players and
good teamwork, the team with the strongest will to win
will prevail.

I have remembered that advice, and it has been a
guiding principle in developing and managing HP. Get
the best people, stress the importance of teamwork, and
get them fired up to win the game.

Stanford University

In the summer of 1929, between my junior and senior
years in high school, my mother, sister, and I drove out
to California. We spent a few weeks in Hermosa Beach
near Los Angeles, and then visited the Neff family in
Palo Alto. We also visited Monterey and Pacific Grove.
Mrs. Neff had been my mother's classmate at Colorado
College, and her oldest daughter, Alice, had just finished her first year at Stanford. Alice took me on a tour
of the Stanford campus. Though I had known nothing
about the university, I was impressed by my visit and
learned that Stanford had a very good electrical engineering program. So I applied in the spring of 1930.
Despite my father's interest in my following him into a
career in law, I had decided as far back as grade school

that I wanted to be an engineer. And, because of my interest in radio and electrical devices, I had narrowed that to electrical engineering.

Admission to Stanford

The University of Colorado at Boulder had a good program in electrical engineering at the time. Some of my older friends were already in the program, so I had assumed that's where I'd go as well. But visiting Stanford changed my mind, and much to my surprise, my application was accepted. The tuition was $114 a quarter, not an insignificant sum in those days of a deepening depression. My father had been appointed a bankruptcy referee in 1929, so my parents were able to provide some financial support and I worked to earn the balance.

My undergraduate years at Stanford were busy. In addition to my studies, I participated in athletics. As a freshman I won letters in football, basketball, and track, and set a school record for scoring the most points in a freshman track meet with our archrival, the University of California. But I decided not to continue with track. It took too much time from my studies, and I had come to Stanford to be a student, not an athlete. I remember that the varsity track coach, Dink Templeton, was very upset with my decision.

Football was not my best sport, but peer pressure was so strong that I played football through my senior year.

That experience reinforced my ideas on how to build a winning team.

While I was attending Stanford, I returned to Pueblo every summer and found a job there. My father didn't insist that I contribute to the cost of my education, but I felt strongly that I should—and besides, I liked to keep busy.

Dave Packard as an end on the Stanford football team, 1934.

I spent one summer with a hard-rock miner near the road to Cripple Creek, the center of the Colorado gold rush. We drilled holes in the rock by hand with a hammer and a rock drill. The miner set the dynamite with a fuse, and after the explosion I hauled the loose rock out with a wheelbarrow. The miner would send samples for assay, but the value never reached the $4 a ton that was required to make the mine profitable. The price of gold had been set at $16 an ounce by President Roosevelt. At today's price of gold the mine probably would have been profitable.

Another summer I had a higher-paying job at a brickyard in Pueblo. The job was to load and unload the kilns. The bricks would be unloaded from the kilns when they were just cool enough to be handled with heavy gloves. By noontime the outside temperature had usually reached a hundred degrees or more. It was a tough job that deserved my higher pay.

I also worked for a construction company, building a road over Wolf Creek Pass in the southwestern corner of Colorado. This was hard work, too, but it had the compensation of an hour or so of good fishing after dinner. My extensive knowledge of this part of the state prompted Bill Hewlett and me to take a long pack trip up the Los Pinos River in the summer of 1934 after we graduated from Stanford.

Yet another summer I had a job delivering ice in the Bessemer area of Pueblo. I would pick up several tons of ice from a freight car that came from Salida, where the ice had been cut and stored during the winter. Since the ice was in large blocks, I had to cut it into pieces for my customers. This was about a year before the repeal of Prohibition, and my most important customers were the beer joints heavily frequented by steel mill workers in the tough part of Pueblo that I had avoided when I was in high school. I had to sell the ice for cash to be able to buy another supply of ice the next day. I can't recall how much money I made that summer, but I believe I did pretty well.

Back at Stanford, it was ham radio that helped set my future course. The university had an amateur radio station in a small building just off the engineering corner of the Quad. It was near the laboratory of a new young professor named Fred Terman. I didn't know much about him at the time, not even that his father was a famous educator and inventor of the well-known Stanford-Binet intelligence test. I would occasionally spend time at the radio station, and Professor Terman would stop by from time to time to visit with me. Finally, on a spring day in 1933, he invited me into his office and suggested I take his graduate course in radio engineering during my senior year. That was the beginning of a series of events that resulted in the establishment of the Hewlett-Packard Company.

As the first undergraduate to be invited into Terman's graduate course, I felt very honored. It was that class, taught by a now legendary teacher, that really sparked my enthusiasm for electronics. The syllabus for the course served as the basis for Terman's famous textbook, *Radio Engineering*, the most influential text on the subject at that time. Professor Terman had the unique ability to make a very complex problem seem the essence of simplicity. This was the secret of his textbook and the reason the book became the most widely used text on the subject in the world. It was a difficult class and a demanding year, especially because I was playing on the varsity football team at the time, carrying a full undergraduate class load, and slinging hash at my fraternity and later at a cafeteria in Palo Alto.

While involved in these various activities I made a number of friends; one of them was Bill Hewlett.

Chapter 2

Friendship with Hewlett

BILL HEWLETT AND I met in the fall of 1930 when we enrolled as freshmen at Stanford. I had already decided that I wanted to be an electrical engineer. Bill hadn't decided on a career, but during our freshman and sophomore years we were in many of the same math and science classes. It wasn't until we were seniors that we became better acquainted, and by the end of that year we had formed a close friendship.

Bill's early years were quite different from mine. His grandparents on both sides of his family lived in California well before the turn of the century, and his mother and father both grew up in San Francisco. His father was a doctor who had trained at Johns Hopkins and who, early in his career, taught medicine at the University of Michigan. It was at Ann Arbor that Bill was born in 1913. A few years later his father became a professor at the Stanford Medical School, which in those days was in San Francisco.

Bill has described his childhood as "busy and happy."

His parents were well educated and fairly well off. Family vacations were usually spent in the Sierra Nevada, where Bill, like me, began to develop a love for the outdoors, which he retains to this day.

As a youngster, Bill gave early evidence of what became a prominent trait: an insatiable curiosity. He wanted to know how things worked and why they did what they did, and he often conducted homemade experiments to find out. Some involved explosives, and like me, he was lucky to survive. He also liked to explore, occasionally climbing rooftops or seeking out areas of San Francisco that were still undeveloped. One of his favorites was the site of the 1915 World's Fair in the Marina district. The remains of the fair—some vacant buildings—provided a wonderful though officially off-limits playground for Bill and his buddies.

Bill went to a private elementary school, going to and from on a cable car. He did well with numbers and arithmetic but had great difficulty reading. He was thought to be a slow learner when, in actuality, he was dyslexic. But in those days no one knew what dyslexia was. He continued to have trouble reading and writing, and later on, in lecture classes, he couldn't write notes fast enough to keep up with the lecturer. So, as is the case with many dyslexics, he learned how to *listen*, to file thoughts and information in a logical form and have them readily available from memory. "This procedure worked particularly well in learning math and science," he says.

When Bill was just twelve, his father died of a brain

tumor and his grandmother and mother took Bill and his sister to Europe. They were in Europe for fifteen months, during which time Louise, Bill's sister, went to school in Paris and Bill was tutored by his mother and grandmother. They also traveled extensively, which in itself was a good education for Bill.

After returning to San Francisco, Bill attended Lowell High School, which was a noted college-preparatory high school. He was an exceptional student in the sciences and an indifferent scholar in almost everything else. In fact, Bill likes to tell the story that when it came time to graduate, he, like many of his classmates, asked his high school principal for a recommen-

Bill Hewlett rappelling on Mt. Owen, California, 1930.

dation to Stanford. The principal called his mother in and said, "Mrs. Hewlett, your son has indicated he wants to go to Stanford. There's nothing in his record to justify my recommending him. Do you know why he wants to go?" She said, "His father taught there." The principal brightened and asked, "Was his father Albion Walter Hewlett?" She said yes, and he said, "He was the finest student I ever had!" That, according to Bill, was how he got in. He added that the next year the principal retired, "So I just made it!"

While in high school, Bill was involved in a number of activities. He enjoyed chemistry and physics and continued experimenting and building things. He built a Tesla coil, made an electric arc from carbon rods, and built a small crystal radio set for himself and another for his sister. He and some other math students talked their teacher into teaching them calculus, which was not a standard high school course. It gave them a running start in college.

Bill has often said that if his father hadn't died, he might have chosen a career in medicine. He has joked that he chose electrical engineering as a college major because he liked electric trains, but certainly in those early years his interests were as much in chemistry and mathematics as in electricity.

Through Bill I became friendly with Ed Porter, Bill's closest boyhood friend. Porter, who came down to Stanford with Bill, was an early ham radio zealot. Since his call letters were W6 BOA, "Frisco Snake" became his ham ID. Ed knew so much about radios that he partially supported himself at Stanford by repairing them. The son of an Episcopal bishop, Ed was a dynamic character who was to play an important role in our lives for the next forty years. His father was the minister who married Bill and Flora Hewlett in 1939 and, prior to his death, baptized three of their five children and all four of my wife Lu's and mine.

There was also in Terman's graduate class a young man named Barney Oliver. He had just transferred to Stanford from Cal Tech as a junior, having already taken most of the required engineering classes. So Terman let him take the graduate class on the stipulation that if Barney didn't pass the first midterm examination, he'd have to drop out. In fact, he got the highest grade not only on the midterm but on every exam for the rest of the year.

Forming a Nucleus

Largely because of Terman's classes, the four of us— Hewlett, Porter, Oliver, and I—became fast friends. It is not a coincidence that a few years later this group would become the management team of Hewlett-Packard. Porter, who died in 1976, spent thirty years at the company as production manager. Oliver, one of the greatest applied scientists of this century, retired in 1981 as HP's director of research and development, and now devotes his energies to such projects as SETI, the search for extraterrestrial intelligence.

Bill Hewlett's and my common interest in the outdoors first manifested itself in our junior year, when one of our professors organized a field trip to the Sierra Nevada to visit a hydroelectric power plant operated by Southern California Edison. Bill and I took that occasion to go fishing and had a wonderful time. That was a precursor of many trips to the mountains, including a two-week pack trip in Colorado shortly after we graduated in 1934. On that occasion we, plus a horse we rented for a dollar a day, hiked up into the San Juan Mountains. There is no question that a shared love of the outdoors strengthened our friendship and helped build a mutual understanding and respect that is at the core of our successful business relationship lasting more than a half century.

Fred Terman's keen interest in radio engineering induced him to become acquainted with almost all of the pioneers in the industry, many of whom were located in the Palo Alto area. Early wireless work by Stanford graduate Cyril F. Elwell was organized into the Federal Telegraph Company at the beginning of the century. Lee De Forest invented the vacuum tube in Palo Alto in 1908, and Fritz Kolster developed the radio direction finder in the 1920s.

In the early 1920s many Bay Area firms moved to Chicago, which had become the center of the radio industry. In 1932 Federal Telegraph moved east to New Jersey. But a lot of people didn't want to move. They opted instead to stay in the area and start their own technology firms. In the 1930s Terman's graduate course in radio engineering included visits to some of these firms. I remember visiting Kaar Engineering in

Palo Alto, Eitel-McCullough in Burlingame, and Charlie Litton's shop, which would in time become Litton Industries in Redwood City. I also went to San Francisco to meet Philo Farnsworth, who was developing a television camera tube.

I remember Terman saying something like: "Well, as you can see, most of these successful radio firms were built by people without much education," adding that business opportunities were even greater for someone with a sound theoretical background in the field. That got us thinking, and in our senior year, with Terman's encouragement, Bill Hewlett, Ed Porter, Barney Oliver, and I were making tentative plans to try to do something on our own after graduation. But our plans were set aside when, in the spring of 1934, I received a job offer from General Electric. The country was then in the throes of the Great Depression and jobs were scarce. Terman encouraged me to take the GE job, pointing out that I would learn a great deal that would prove useful in our own endeavor. He also thought Bill would benefit from some graduate work. So we agreed to postpone our business venture, still determined eventually to start the company we had talked about.

Experience at General Electric

Since my job at General Electric did not start until February 1935, I decided to take some fall-quarter courses at the University of Colorado in Boulder. The best course was one in engineering mathematics taught by a Professor Hutchison. He could put two columns of five-digit numbers of about twenty lines on the blackboard and add both columns faster than anyone in the class could add one. I found his course to be one of the most interesting I had ever taken.

In January 1935, I drove my mother and sister east to visit some friends in Pittsburgh. Then I drove up to Schenectady to begin my job with GE. On my first day I met with a Mr. Boring, who had interviewed me at Stanford. He knew of my interest in electronics (still called "radio") but told me there was no future for electronics at General Electric and recommended that I concentrate my work and interests on generators, motors, and other heavy components for public utility plants and electrical transmission systems.

I have often thought of the irony of Mr. Boring's advice because our electronics firm, Hewlett-Packard Company, has become larger than the entire General Electric Company was at the time he gave me that advice.

GE continued its policy, even during the depression, of hiring some college graduates each year and initially putting them to work in various test departments. My first assignment was in refrigerator products, testing refrigerators for leaks and other problems. It was on the swing shift and was not very interesting.

I decided to look for another job on my own and found one first in the radio transmitter department, testing equipment being built for the army. That was not very challenging either, so I looked around further and found a job in the vacuum-tube engineering department. It was in the same building as GE's main research department. This new job was interesting, and I had a chance as well to meet some bright people from the main research laboratory.

My initial assignment was in the section where they were making controlled mercury-vapor rectifier tubes for the control of spot and seam welding. The largest tube was a glass bulb about the size of a gallon jug, with the anode held by a seal at the top and the mercury pool connected by a seal through the bottom. The control element was a pointed piece of silicon carbide connected by a seal and a lead on one side of the tube. The arc was started on each positive cycle during the control period and could be controlled to a fraction of a cycle. If the control element lost control, the tube blew up!

The test facility was on the ground floor of the building, and there were two large warehouse doors that were left open whenever a test was under way. The tube was protected with a strong metal-mesh shield. It contained the glass splinters if a tube exploded, but the mercury pool became a cloud of mercury vapor that drifted out of the room through the open doors. The operator had to run through the doors ahead of the mercury vapor and wait for it to disperse before entering the room again.

These tubes were made in batches of twenty, and every tube in the last batch had failed when I was given the job of getting the next batch through.

Working Together

I learned everything I could about possible causes of failure, and I decided to spend most of my time on the factory floor to make sure every step was done properly. It soon became apparent that the instructions the engineering department gave the factory people were not adequate to ensure that every step would be done properly. I found the factory people eager to do the job right. We worked together to conduct tests and identify every possible cause of failure, and as a result, every tube in that batch of twenty passed its final test without a single failure.

That was a very important lesson for me—that personal communication was often necessary to back up written instructions. That was the genesis of what became "management by walking around" at the Hewlett-Packard Company.

In those days my GE friends and I were each earning less than $90 per month, so five or six of us rented a large house and hired a housekeeper. Since we could live on a dollar per day, we had quite a bit left for everything else. One could buy a fairly good suit for $25 and, even with a low salary, could actually save a few dollars each month.

I enjoyed my experience at GE. I was able to learn many things that later proved helpful when we started our own business, and I also developed close friendships with some individuals who would later make their own mark in electronics. One was Bobby Wilson, who had graduated from Yale and spent his first year out of school as a radio operator and navigator on a flight around the world in a private plane operated by a Dr. Light. Bobby ended up managing GE's X-ray division in Chicago. Then there was Jack Hutchins, who presented a paper with me at a meeting of the American Institute of Electrical Engineers in New York City in the spring of 1936. Jack later formed his own business in Illinois making high-power transistors.

Another fellow who lived in our house in Schenectady was John Fluke, with whom I developed a lifelong friendship. During World War II John worked for Admiral Hyman Rickover in Washington, and after the war he started his own company in the Northwest—the John Fluke Manufacturing Company, a major producer of electronic instruments. Through John I met Admiral Rickover, who was very helpful to me when I went to Washington in 1969 as deputy secretary of defense.

John Cage was another GE friend who was later to play an important role at HP. After the war, John was an electronics professor at Purdue University. I would call and ask him about graduating engineers we might want to hire. He recommended a number of outstanding people to us. In 1956 we hired John to supervise an important product-development project, and later he organized and managed Hewlett-Packard Ltd., our first British subsidiary. In 1971 he co-edited with Barney

Oliver a textbook, *Electronic Measurement and Instrumentation.*

In 1936, still gripped by the depression, GE reduced some of its work schedules, and many of us got off work at three in the afternoon. This allowed time for golf—or in my case, basketball. I liked the game and eventually joined a local professional team. We practiced in the evenings, and on the weekends we played games in some of the small towns around northern New York and New England. We made only a few dollars a week, not a princely sum but still very useful in those economically depressed times. We played our last game of the season in New York City at the Thirty-fourth Street Armory. I don't remember much about the game except that our team lost and that Kate Smith, a popular singer, tossed the ball to start the game.

While I was in Schenectady, Bill Hewlett was busy doing graduate work. He completed a year at Stanford in 1935, then spent the following year getting a master's degree at MIT. While in Cambridge he managed to visit me in Schenectady a few times, and we were able to take some canoe trips together.

I enjoyed my stay in Schenectady and spent many weekends fishing in the lakes of northern New York, Vermont, and New Hampshire. In the fall the woods were beautiful, and some GE friends and I would hunt deer, woodcock, and other game.

In the winter I spent many weekends skiing at North Creek, New York. Skiing was just beginning to be a

Dave Packard skiing at Gore Mountain, New York, 1936.

popular sport. The people in North Creek used their school buses to take skiers to the top of Gore Mountain. There were numerous trails down the mountain for beginners and experts. Skis were made of either hickory, maple, or ash, and I broke three pairs of skis missing turns on the trails and going off into the woods. Fortunately my legs were stronger than the skis! These trips engendered great camaraderie among the recent college graduates working in Schenectady.

In 1937 I drove back across the country to Palo Alto. I had a sleeping bag with me, so I didn't have to stop at any hotels. In those days it was perfectly safe to sleep at any convenient place along the highway. By then Bill had returned from the East, and I wanted to spend some time with him. The primary purpose of my visit, however, was to see a young woman named Lucile Salter. I had first met Lu during my senior year at Stanford while I was serving meals in her sorority dining room.

One weekend in the spring of 1934, a group of my friends were organizing a trip up to San Francisco to go dancing on Saturday night at the Mark. I didn't have a date, but a friend of mine thought he knew a young woman at Delta Gamma—where I had a kitchen job—who would probably agree to go with me. There I was in the kitchen, immersed to my elbows in pots and pans, when Lucile strolled up to me and said, "When do you want me?"

Before that dance, I knew Lucile very slightly. She was an attractive and very bright student from San Francisco; our night of dancing blossomed into a romance that continued even after we had graduated and were three thousand miles apart. In the years after our graduation, I had gotten to meet Lu's parents and her sister, Audrey, who was also a student at Stanford. After a while Lu and I began to contemplate marriage fairly seriously.

During my visit to Palo Alto I also got together with Bill Hewlett, and at that time we had our first "official" business meeting. The minutes of the meeting, dated August 23, 1937, are headed "tentative organization plans and a tentative work program for a proposed business venture." The product ideas we discussed included high-frequency receivers and medical equipment, and it was noted that "we should make every attempt to keep up on [the newly announced technology of] television." Our proposed name for the new company: The Engineering Service Company.

By the spring of 1938 Lu and I had decided to get married. She resigned her job as secretary to the Stanford registrar and took the Overland Express to Chicago, changing trains there to reach Schenectady. It was a four-day journey. It is a measure of how scarce jobs were at the time that I didn't dare take time off from GE and risk losing my higher-paying job. I didn't want the people at GE to have any indication that I didn't plan to come back. For that reason, I only took off Friday afternoon so we could get married, spend our honeymoon over the weekend in Montreal, and I could be back at work Monday morning.

During those months Fred Terman had been thinking about how Bill and I might proceed, and in the summer of 1938 he arranged a Stanford fellowship for me. It carried a stipend of $500 a year, but more important, it reunited me with Hewlett. The fellowship offered an interesting technical challenge. I was to work with a young Stanford inventor, Russ Varian, on one of his ideas. The task was to modify a vacuum tube to operate at higher frequencies. It was one part of a larger project that would make Russ and his brother Sig famous: the klystron tube, the technology behind radar and particle accelerators.

My bosses at GE gave me their blessing and an

Lucile Packard, as the Packards are about to leave Schenectady to drive cross-country to California in 1938.

unpaid leave of absence, and in August Lu and I drove back to California with a used Sears, Roebuck drill press in the rumble seat. It would be HP's first piece of equipment.

I didn't formally resign from GE until nearly a year later. Lucile always remembered the moment she dropped my letter of resignation in the mailbox in June 1939. Mailing that letter cut our financial ties. But we were hopeful and excited about what the future had in store.

Terman had arranged for me to do the laboratory work on the Varian research project up at Charlie Litton's place, Litton Engineering Laboratories, in Redwood City. He had also arranged for me to get credit for my work at GE so that I could get my EE degree from Stanford with just one year of residence.

Lu got her job back at the Stanford registrar's office. Working Monday through Friday and half of Saturday, she essentially supported us for the next few years. But, most important, Hewlett was back in town as well. During the interim, he had obtained his master's degree from MIT and upon graduation had exactly one job offer, with Jensen Speaker in Chicago. But Terman came through for him too, putting Bill together with a San Francisco doctor who was interested in developing some medical equipment.

Chapter 3

Garage Becomes Workshop

NOW THAT BILL AND I were back together, we started putting our plans to work. Bill had found a two-story house on Addison Avenue in Palo Alto, and Lu and I rented the lower floor. Bill, who at the time was still a bachelor, lived in a little building out back. There was also a one-car garage, and that became our workshop. (Editor's note: In 1989 the state of California designated the Addison Avenue garage as a California Historical Landmark and "the birthplace of Silicon Valley.")

Beginning in the autumn of 1938, my schedule was to go to classes at Stanford most mornings, work with Bill and also find time to study in the afternoon, then go up to Litton Laboratories in the evening. It helped that Charlie Litton didn't like getting started early in the day, but instead worked until 2:00 or 3:00 A.M. Otherwise, I'm not sure how I could have juggled all this work and study and still have had time for a home life.

With my experience at GE and with Charlie's help, I was quite capable of making the vacuum-tube models to test Russ Varian's theories. My relationship with Charlie developed into a long and enduring friendship. Charlie was able to do everything better than anyone else. In the fall of 1938, when he wanted to build a new plant, he didn't hire a contractor to do the excavating. Instead, he bought a Caterpillar loader and excavated the site himself. I helped him and became fairly proficient with a bulldozer. When Bill Hewlett and I acquired a ranch in 1954, I bought a bulldozer and helped build more than twenty miles of roads.

Dave Packard building the roads at San Felipe ranch near San Jose, California, 1955.

Charlie Litton had started with the Federal Telegraph Company in Palo Alto. But when Sothenes Behn, who ran Federal Telegraph with his brother Hernand, moved the company to New Jersey in 1932, Charlie decided to set up his own manufacturing company. He thought the vacuum-tube manufacturing equipment that was on the market was not good enough, so he decided to design and manufacture his own glass-blowing lathes for the big 50-kilowatt tubes that were used by radio transmitters. He no sooner made his first lathe when RCA bought it; his second was immediately bought by Westinghouse.

Litton Answers the Call

Most of the people around the country doing vacuum-tube work knew about Charlie's activity, and ordered his new designs. His most important contribution was the design of a low-vapor pressure-oil, all-metal vacuum pump. Up until then most of the vacuum pumps had been mercury vapor pumps, such as the pumps I used at GE. These had the disadvantage of requiring that the mercury vapor traps be cooled by liquid air. Sources of low-vapor pressure oil in the country were very limited, but Charlie had discovered that by distilling a certain commercial brand of motor oil he could produce his own low-vapor pressure oil.

In 1939, at the urging of physicists Albert Einstein and Leo Szilard, President Roosevelt established an enterprise to produce an atomic explosion using uranium fission. The people involved in this undertaking, later known as the Manhattan Project, decided to use a process requiring a large volume of low-vapor pressure oil. And they decided that Charlie could produce the oil quicker and better than anyone else. In a typically Litton manner, he ordered the largest redwood water tank available, set it up in three or four weeks, and installed the stills. The motor oil was delivered in railroad tank cars to Redwood City, and then Charlie distilled it in his water-tank building. Although I had not been cleared to know about the project, I was working so closely with Charlie that I knew all about it.

Charlie's talents also extended to the four-wheel drive; he was the first person to use a four-wheel-drive vehicle to explore the Sierra Nevada. He constructed his own by linking two light-truck chassis, each with a motor and a transmission to power two of its wheels. After the war he was among the first to recognize how effective a Jeep could be in maneuvering in the Sierra. Bill and I bought a Jeep and on our first trip—in the Desolation Valley area—we got stuck on a rock with all four wheels off the ground. It took a little time to build up rocks under the wheels and get going again. We bought a stake truck large enough to carry the Jeep, a trailer to follow the truck, and a station wagon with the back fitted out to sleep in. Every year a group of us, including Noel Eldred, Dave Scott, Ray Demere, Bill Hewlett, and myself, went on a deer-hunting trip in Nevada or Montana for two weeks. As a result, a close friendship developed among Bill Hewlett and me, Noel Eldred, and the other people from the company who went with us. We always got two deer each and sometimes an elk.

During those months in 1938 when Bill and I were getting started in our Palo Alto garage, we were in frequent contact with our Stanford classmate and close friend, Ed Porter. Ed had been selling air-conditioning equipment, primarily to hotels in the Sacramento Valley, and by now was doing well enough that he decided to stay in the valley rather than join Bill and me. But Ed did ask us to design some custom-control equipment for his air conditioners.

In the fall of 1938, we had not yet decided on what products we should develop and manufacture, and so we did a number of jobs that came to our attention. T. I. Moseley was a local entrepreneur and president of his own company, Dalmo-Victor; he came to us with a number of ideas for products in our early days. At one point, he even decided to produce harmonicas.

Moseley knew about an audio oscillator Bill had developed, and he asked us to produce a tuner for his harmonica using this oscillator. It turned out that the oscillator was not nearly accurate enough to do this. I don't remember what ever came of Moseley's harmonicas.

Moseley also was trying to develop an exerciser using electrical pulses to activate the muscles. He had an accommodating wife, and we spent one Sunday applying electrical currents of different frequencies to activate her leg muscles. Neither of Moseley's projects was put into production, but his assignments provided a little income for Bill and me.

We designed and built a variable-frequency motor controller for the Lick Observatory atop nearby Mount Hamilton; our controller enabled the telescope to track accurately. We also invented a signaling device to indicate a foul-line roll for a local bowling alley.

These miscellaneous jobs made us more sure of ourselves and our skills. They also revealed something we hadn't planned but that was of great benefit to our partnership—namely, that our abilities tended to be complementary. Bill was better trained in circuit technology, and I was better trained and more experienced in manufacturing processes. This combination of abilities was particularly useful in designing and manufacturing electronic products.

From our efforts in building various devices we'd made a little money, and in the back of our minds was growing the notion that just maybe one of these devices could be developed into a viable product. In recognition of our progress, small as it was, Bill and I began 1939 by signing a partnership agreement. I don't remember the exact terms of the agreement, but I know it was pretty informal. Bill advanced some money to buy some components and tools, and I contributed the equipment I brought from Schenectady. We flipped a coin to see whose name would come first in the company name. Needless to say, Bill won.

Fred Terman was once again behind the next step.

Back in 1927 a Bell Labs scientist named Harold Black had written a paper about a new idea called "negative feedback." It was ideal for telephone "repeaters," or amplifiers, because by using this technique, the gain of an amplifier could be made relatively independent of changes in the characteristics of the vacuum tube involved. For the same reason, it became useful in electronic measuring instruments. In the spring of 1938, working in Terman's laboratory, a group of students, including Bill Hewlett, developed some laboratory-equipment applications for negative feedback. Bill's important contribution was the resistance-stabilized audio oscillator. Terman also made an important contribution. By using some approximations he reduced the Black equations to a simpler form that was much easier to use.

Bill's audio oscillator represented the first practical, low-cost method of generating high-quality audio frequencies needed in communications, geophysics, medicine, and defense work. The audio oscillator was to become the Hewlett-Packard Company's first product.

Later that year, after we started up in the garage, Terman arranged for Harold Buttner, an engineering graduate of Stanford and International Telephone and Telegraph's vice president of research and development, to take a look at Bill's oscillator. Buttner was so impressed that he offered us $500 for the foreign patent rights and help in getting the U.S. patent.

In November, we built a model of the audio oscillator, and Bill took it up to Portland, Oregon, to an

Institute of Radio Engineers conference. The response was positive enough that we decided to make a run for it. We built the first production model by Christmas, and I clearly recall having this unit sitting on the mantel above the fireplace. There we took pictures of it and produced a two-page sales brochure that we sent to a list of about twenty-five potential customers provided by Fred Terman.

We designated this first product the Model 200A because we thought the name would make us look like we'd been around for a while. We were afraid that if people knew we'd never actually developed, designed, and built a finished product, they'd be scared off. Our pricing was even more naive: We set it at $54.40 not because of any cost calculations but because, of all things, it reminded us of "54°40' or Fight!" (the 1844 slogan used in the campaign to establish the northern border of the United States in the Pacific Northwest). We soon discovered we couldn't afford to build the machines for that price. Luckily, our nearest competition was a $400 oscillator from General Radio, which gave us considerable room to maneuver.

We weren't expecting much from our first mailing, but amazingly enough, in the first couple of weeks of January back came several orders . . . and some were accompanied by checks.

Charlie Litton was a tremendous help in getting us started in production. He gave us access to his shop so we could do things we weren't able to accomplish in the garage on our own. Using Charlie's foundry, I had made the patterns and cast the aluminum parts for the air-conditioning control devices we supplied Ed Porter. Litton also had an engraving machine, so we'd been able to engrave the hotel names on the controls.

Fabricating Instrument Panels

When we started making the audio oscillators, we bought the cabinets but made the panels ourselves. We sawed them out of aluminum and drilled the holes. Then we'd spraypaint them at home and use the kitchen oven to bake on the paint. Then I'd take the panels up to Charlie's and engrave all the designations on the panels through the paint. Next, we calibrated the dials by setting up a frequency standard. Then we marked the dial with a pencil and I'd go back up to Charlie's and engrave those pencil lines. In the beginning, each of the oscillators was individually calibrated. There were always a few tricks involved in using the engraving equipment, and Charlie knew them all.

I suppose we could have eventually done many of these things on our own. But having Charlie Litton and his equipment there made an important difference during a period when time and money were very tight. He never saw us as competitors but always as compatriots.

Charlie did something else important as well. He loved to expound and philosophize on new ideas. And whenever he wanted to learn more about something, he'd organize a seminar at his shop and invite me and a few other people, usually from Stanford. Among this group was Alex Poniatoff, who later founded Ampex Corporation. The seminars occurred several times during 1938. I can remember a number of discussions about physical phenomena such as wave theory and quantum mechanics. We also talked about business philosophy. Charlie was very conservative in this regard. As eccentric as he was, he knew you had to support your company and pay your bills. I learned a lot about running a business from those conversations.

I also gained a lot from two classes I took at Stanford that fall of 1938: business law and management accounting. I had signed up because I thought they might be of some use in our new business. Looking back, they were among the most important courses I ever took, because the first taught me enough about partnerships, contracts, and incorporation so that for the next few years we rarely required the services of lawyers; and the second helped me set up the books and, with Lu's help in the evenings and on Sundays, keep them balanced.

The Disney Sale: Myths and Facts

When Bill Hewlett took the original model of the audio oscillator to the technical conference in Portland in November 1938, he showed it to several people. Among those who expressed considerable interest in it was Bud Hawkins, the chief sound engineer from Walt

Disney Studios. Hawkins was developing the sound equipment for Disney's innovative movie *Fantasia* and was planning to buy, for $400 each, audio oscillators from the General Radio Company. When Bill told him our model would cost less than $100, Hawkins decided to buy our oscillators instead of General Radio's. In the end, after Hawkins had us make enough modifications in the original design for the result to be the Model 200B, he ordered eight units at $71.50 each.

Through the years there has been considerable overstatement about this sale to Disney. Contrary to some views, HP did not make a technical contribution to the production of *Fantasia*. Instead, we enabled Disney to buy a good product at a price considerably less than our competitor's. It's also been said that if it hadn't been for our sale to Disney, we might have gone out of business. The truth of the matter is that with or without the Disney sale, Bill and I were determined to move ahead with our company.

Another gentleman who took an early interest in our activities and who was destined to play an immensely important role in the success of Hewlett-Packard was Norman Neely. Norm was a Southern California manufacturers' representative handling radio, recording, and other electrical equipment. He had heard about Hewlett's oscillator and invited Bill to speak at the Radio Engineers Club in Los Angeles. The evening did not start out on a promising note, for it began with the club president introducing Bill Hewlett as "Bill Packard," but the presentation itself drew a strong response—none more so than the one from Norm himself.

Shortly thereafter Norm visited Bill and me in our Addison Avenue garage. We had already approached him about being our first sales representative, and during his visit we reached a verbal agreement and sealed it with a handshake. That was the way we were to conduct our business with Norm for the next fifty years.

During our conversation Norm emphasized the importance of our offering more than one product because a single product rarely made a successful company. The products that Bill and his associates had developed at Stanford in the spring of 1938 included a number of instruments designed to make audio-frequency measurements. In addition to Bill's oscillator, we decided to develop a full line of audio-frequency-measuring instruments based on this work. That meant we would be in direct competition with the General Radio Company.

At the end of 1939, our first full year in business, our sales totaled $5,369 and we had made $1,563 in profits. We would show a profit every year thereafter.

Chapter 4

Gaining More Space

BY THE FALL OF 1939 our business had grown to the point where we needed additional space. So we rented a small building in Palo Alto on Page Mill Road near El Camino Real, behind the workshop of John "Tinker" Bell and about two miles from the garage. About that same time Bill Hewlett married Flora Lamson, whom he had first met when they were children and their families were vacationing in the Sierra. Bill was more than happy to give up his tiny one-room bachelor quarters on Addison Avenue to move into a house with Flora not far from our new shop.

We set up an office in the front section of our new building, while the back room held a few machine tools and assembly benches. There were also facilities for hot dipping and painting. It seemed as if we had all the space we would ever need.

Not that our new location was without its problems. In the winter when it rained, water would run down Page Mill Road, and occasionally we'd have to sandbag

Bill and Flora Hewlett at Squaw Valley for the opening of the 1960 Winter Olympics.

the front door to keep the water out. To replace Lu's kitchen oven, which we had used to bake paint onto our cabinets, we built an oven out of an old refrigerator and had it out back behind the shop. Unfortunately, we didn't take into account that the refrigerator had kapok insulation, and one night the thing caught fire. Luckily, somebody was driving by, saw the flames, and called the fire department before much damage was done.

In those early days Bill and I had to be versatile. We had to tackle almost everything ourselves—from inventing and building products to pricing, packaging, and shipping them; from dealing with customers and sales representatives to keeping the books; from writing the ads to sweeping up at the end of the day. Many of the things I learned in this process were invaluable, and not available in business schools.

We found that parts for our products were priced on a two-level structure. Manufacturers' representatives sold to retail dealers at the factory price, and then the retail dealers marked up the parts ten times for sale to their customers. We got acquainted with the Allen-Bradley representative, Bill Purdy, who set us up to buy at factory prices. We later were able to work out the same arrangement for other components, and thus could buy most of our parts at 10 percent of the retail price. Of greater difficulty was obtaining the cabinets and chassis for our products. At the time, the Bay Area had few sheet-metal or mechanical-parts shops. We hired a man named Al Spear to make our cabinets. It was customary in those days to have measurement equipment in wooden cabinets. Most cabinets were made of walnut, but we decided to use oak. As we designed test equipment for higher frequencies, we gave up using wood because it served no useful purpose and added to the cost.

Our sheet-metal work was done by Ernie Shiller, who had a one-man shop just down the street from our Addison Avenue garage. Ernie was a gruff old fellow, but he was a good mechanic and a good craftsman, and he did our sheet-metal work for a number of years.

A Need for Cash

Cash flow was a frequent problem during those early days. I recall that early in 1940 the ITT Company had a contract to build an instrument for an aircraft-landing

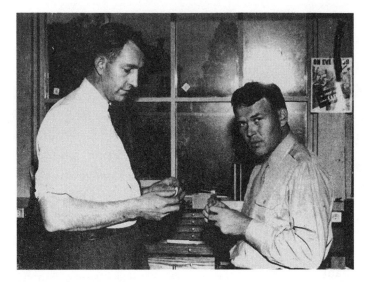

Dave Packard (left) and Bill Hewlett in the shop, 1944.

system. The system required a variable-frequency oscillator and a crystal-controlled, fixed-frequency oscillator. General Radio, a company I mentioned earlier as a supplier of audio oscillators, had provided ITT with the variable-frequency oscillator but shied away from the fixed-frequency version. We agreed to take it on, not knowing any better, and it turned out to be a great challenge. As we started work, it became obvious we didn't have enough engineering talent to complete the job in the time required. Fortunately, I was able to hire Noel Eldred, Bill Doolittle, and Brunton Bauer from Heintz and Kaufman. All three became important members of our team. We managed to build the unit to the required specifications, and we delivered it to ITT along with our invoice. For some time we didn't get paid, and it got to the point where unless we received payment, we couldn't meet the next week's payroll. So I called Harold Buttner, our friend at ITT, and he immediately wired the funds to me.

Harold was a good friend in a number of ways, and when he retired from ITT, I immediately asked him to join our HP board. He became one of our best directors, and because of his experience at ITT, he knew people at virtually every electronics company in the world.

Our experience with the ITT contract convinced me that we needed more working capital. I concluded that the thing to do was to establish some credit with the Bank of America, the largest bank in California. We applied for a loan of $500, and they sent a man out to look us over. He apparently wasn't very impressed, for the bank agreed to give us a loan only if we would sign over to it our accounts receivable.

That didn't have much appeal to us, so I went over to our little local bank, Palo Alto National, and introduced myself to its president, Jud Crary. He said he remembered me as an athlete at Stanford. I described our initial success and explained that we now needed a loan of $500 to expand our business. Crary listened carefully, asked some questions, then wrote out a note for me to sign. We then walked across the room, and he handed me a deposit slip for $500. That little leap of faith on Crary's part was the beginning of a long and happy relationship between us. And when we finally grew to the point where our financing requirements were beyond the bank's legal limits, we went to Palo Alto National's associate bank, Wells Fargo. The Wells Fargo Bank sent a retired engineer to visit us. I spent a full afternoon with him and I have remembered ever since some advice he gave me. He said that more businesses die from indigestion than starvation. I have observed the truth of that advice many times since then.

In the fall of 1939, shortly after we had moved from the garage to the Page Mill Road building, we had a visit from Melville Eastham, the founder of General Radio. Headquartered in Massachusetts, GenRad, as it is now known, had been established for some time, and Bill and I knew it to be a fine company.

Fred Terman had introduced us to Eastham, who spent an afternoon with us and gave us some very good advice on how to organize and run a company. I knew by then that Eastham realized we were going to be in direct competition with his company, and I anticipated that our meeting with him would be uncomfortable. He assured us, however, that competition was a good thing and it was better to have two companies introducing a new product, especially if it incorporated new technology, because that made it all the more credible to the customer. After that meeting, Eastham and his General Radio colleagues continued to be helpful to us, and although we were competitors, we also became good friends.

During 1940 our little company continued to grow, and by the end of the year we had about ten people on the payroll, including Harvey Zeiber, the first employee we hired when we were still in the garage. We had also added our first secretary, Helen Perry, and we had expanded into the front of Tinker Bell's much larger corner building.

That year, also, Lu and I began to build our family. Our first child, David Woodley, was born that October. Lu had resigned from her job at Stanford but continued to work for the company. She did everything, including interviewing prospective employees.

Dave and Lucile Packard with David Woodley, 1940.

Hewlett Called into the Service

We had appointed Bruce Burlingame as our sales representative on the East Coast, and he was a good friend of the head of the Army Signal Corps laboratories at Fort Monmouth, New Jersey. In the spring of 1941 Bill Hewlett, who had a commission in the army reserves, was called to active duty. With Bruce Burlingame's help we were able to convince the Signal Corps that Bill could contribute more to the defense effort by managing, with me, the important work we were doing at HP. Bill came back in the fall but was on the job only a short time before the Japanese attack on Pearl Harbor on December 7. Soon thereafter, he was called back to duty and spent the duration of the war as an officer in the Army Signal Corps. During those years we were both so busy that we had little contact.

HP was not a defense contractor in the sense of designing and building equipment solely for the military. But since much of our equipment was bought by the military services and by defense contractors, we grew rapidly during the war. Our annual sales volume moved up to a million dollars very quickly, and by the end of the war we employed two hundred people. There was a state employment office in Palo Alto, and we got most of our people through this office. I recall hiring a retired army officer, "Cap" Stuart, and asking him to take over our payroll accounting and the distribution of our payroll expense. He did a very thorough job and made sure that everything balanced down to the last penny.

We also hired a retired mechanical engineer, Rufe Kingman, who turned out to be an expert machinery designer. We took on a major job for the navy that required a servo system to control antenna dishes. Rufe knew what tolerances were required for the bearings, and he did an excellent job designing the gears. He also designed a machine to make plastic cards to hold the components. It formed the terminals from a long brass strip, punched the holes for the terminals, and inserted and locked the terminals. This provided an excellent mount for our components at a very low cost. We used these terminal cards in all our designs until we started using printed circuit boards. We also devised a manual-dexterity test to help us find people who could mount and solder components skillfully. This is a relatively simple operation, but if not done properly, can lead to product failures.

In the early 1940s Sothenes Behn built a major factory in New Jersey, which was designed to manufacture most of the magnetrons for the war effort. It was laid out with wide aisles in the production area so that Behn could comfortably escort the big-brass visitors from Washington. It had only one problem: It couldn't produce even one good tube! In desperation Behn asked Charlie Litton to come back and make the factory work. Charlie agreed. A good administrative man, Jack Copeland, was sent out from New Jersey and put in charge of

Charlie's operation in Redwood City. Jack did not have any technical knowledge or experience, so I offered to help. About a year later a major fire at Litton Engineering Laboratories destroyed much of their machine shop. By that time we at HP had built up a good machine shop in Palo Alto, but we were using it only on the day shift. So I made HP's shop available to Jack and his people at night. That fitted their schedule and enabled them to keep going until they could rebuild and reequip their own plant.

We began operating two shifts of workers during the war, and in 1943 we built our first building at 395 Page Mill Road to accommodate our increased production. Although the pressure to meet production deadlines was enormous, there was also lots of excitement and a

Hewlett-Packard production line, c. 1944.

great sense of camaraderie. We were one of only three California manufacturers to win the army-navy "E" award in 1943. Only 2.5 percent of all manufacturers in the United States were so honored. Our people worked very hard, and we wanted to recognize and encourage their contribution. Even before the war Bill and I had begun implementing an incentive compensation plan for all our people, a plan based on something we'd learned from General Radio. It involved a complicated formula, but in essence it paid everyone a bonus, as a percentage of their base pay, should production exceed certain levels. General Radio's plan applied to engineers only. But Bill and I thought everyone at HP should be included. We wanted to recognize the contributions of each individual, not just a special group.

The plan worked very well and was especially helpful during the war. Wages had been frozen by law, but since plans like this that had already been established could stay in effect, we were able to continue our program of paying bonuses tied to production.

Eventually, because of big gains in productivity, the bonus to our entire workforce rose to as much as 85 percent of base wages. At that point, which was some time after the war, we abandoned this particular bonus plan. But in no way did we discontinue the practice of sharing profits among all our people. To this day, Hewlett-Packard has a profit-sharing program that encourages teamwork and maintains that important link between employee effort and corporate success.

One day early in the war, I came to the office to find

two men from the local Renegotiation Board waiting to see me. Renegotiation was a procedure established by the federal government to prevent companies from making excessive profits from their war efforts. It was a good program under which the government tried to allow a reasonable profit for good performance.

Bill and I had decided we were going to reinvest our profits and not resort to long-term borrowing. I felt very strongly about this issue, and we found we were clearly able to finance 100 percent growth per year by reinvesting our profits. After some discussion with the members of the board, they seemed to be impressed with what we were doing but said they had a limit of 12 percent of profit they could allow on equity. I pointed out that our business had been doubling every year and that it would continue to do so for several years. I also told them that I had kept my salary at a lower level than it should have been because I did not think it was fair for my salary to be higher than Bill's army salary. More-over, I pointed out that we had controlled our costs to the extent that the government could not get better products from anyone else at a lower price. For these reasons I would not accept 12 percent on equity. They said I would have to take my case to Washington. I did so and worked out an agreement with the government that gave our company virtually everything we asked for.

Entry into Microwave

Even though production continued to be our main emphasis, we began to get into product development in the early part of the war when we got acquainted with some people at the Naval Research Laboratory. We were interested in selling them our standard products but also interested in finding out what other instruments they might need. In the course of this relationship we became acquainted with Dr. Andy Haeff, who headed a section of the lab. Dr. Haeff and his associates had developed a microwave signal generator, and they wanted to get additional units built for use by the navy. We had no previous experience in the frequency range, but we agreed to build these units. We had to figure out how to do the manufacturing with our limited machine-shop capability. Norman Shrock was helpful in this project and somehow we got it done and delivered some units within a short time and at a reasonable cost. Dr. Haeff was impressed and asked us to do some further work for the navy. We developed additional instruments, and later on, again working with Dr. Haeff, we built a device his group developed that was capable of jamming an enemy's shipboard radar. It was at the core of what was code-named the Leopard project. We were very conscientious about meeting our delivery schedule on this project, working around the clock. I recall moving a cot into the factory and sleeping there many nights.

This activity was important to us. We acquired some new technical knowledge that helped get us into the forefront of the microwave instrumentation business, a move that paid handsome dividends for the company after the war.

As our company grew during World War II, so did our line of products. Following on the heels of Bill's audio oscillator, we designed a wave analyzer and some distortion analyzers. We then developed a higher-power audio-signal generator. This found a particularly good market in the manufacture of proximity fuses for the military. We did not build a vacuum-tube voltmeter at this time because one was being built by the Balantine Company, whose products were handled by most of the same sales representatives handling our products. It turned out that the Balantine product had some deficiencies, and so later on we developed our Model 400A vacuum-tube voltmeter, which became a very successful product.

Maintaining a Focus

Though these instruments differed from one another, all were designed to measure and test electronic equipment. They reflected our strategy to concentrate on building a group of complementary products rather than becoming involved in a lot of unrelated things. I believe this decision to focus our efforts was extremely important, not only in the early days of the company but later on as well. During the war, for example, we could have taken on some big—at least for us—production contracts. But that would have built the company to a level that probably couldn't be sustained later on. I felt that we should take on no more than we could reasonably handle, building a solid base by doing what we did best—designing and manufacturing high-quality instruments.

Of course, several electronics companies in California were capable of and interested in taking on war-related contracts. Some of them felt, at least in the early days of the war, that they were not getting their fair share of these contracts. Their discontent helped fuel the formation of the West Coast Electronics Manufacturers Association. This association provided a vehicle for West Coast companies to band together and make their case in Washington. Originally, there were about a dozen members in Southern California, organized by Les Hoffman of Mission Bell Radio, later to become Hoffman Radio. I put together a similar group in the North, including Eitel-McCullough, Heintz and Kaufman, Kaar Engineering, and HP. As our industry grew, so did the association. In the late 1950s it became WEMA, representing the interests and concerns of electronics companies west of the Mississippi. In 1978 the name was changed to the American Electronics Association (AEA). Today the AEA is a national trade association with more than 3,400 member organizations throughout the country.

In 1945, after the war ended, Bill returned to Palo

Alto, just in time for Christmas. Soon he was back in stride at the company. Some of his experiences as a Signal Corps officer proved to be quite useful, involving him in various scientific and engineering projects. He became acquainted with a number of technical people, some of whom we later hired into the company.

War's end brought some worrisome problems to most companies and we were not immune. As expected, there was a sharp decline in our business and a corresponding drop in employment. Many women who had joined us as war-production workers left the company after the war was over. We managed to retain our key people, however, and the slowdown gave us the opportunity to seek out and attract some good technical people to the company. We were especially interested in some of the engineers who had worked during the war with Fred Terman at Harvard's Radio Research Laboratory and at other war-related research labs. As it turned out, we were able to hire Ralph Lee, Bruce Wholey, Art Fong, Ray Demere, and Howard Zeidler. And, some time later, George Kan and Horace Overacker. These engineers were instrumental in developing some much-needed new products during the critical postwar period . . . and, in the longer run, filling essential positions within the company.

I mentioned that some work we did for the navy during the war had given us the opportunity to build some microwave signal generators. From that beginning we had acquired quite a bit of expertise in microwave equipment, and following the war, we decided to continue in the field of microwave. It's interesting to note that General Radio, at that time the leading instrument company, didn't think there was much future in microwave test equipment. But it turned out to represent an important and growing share of our business. Along the way we had heard that Varian Associates, which had a small waveguide business, wanted to devote its attention to other things, and so, in 1950, we purchased Varian's waveguide business and folded it into our other microwave operations.

If Hewlett-Packard was growing during the 1940s and 1950s, so was the Packard family: Our three daughters, Nancy, Susan, and Julie, were born in 1943, 1946, and 1953, respectively. To accommodate these children, Lucile and I were obliged to move several times. After leaving the house on Addison, we moved to a house on Matadero in south Palo Alto, which was just across a vacant field from the Tinker Bell shop. A few years later, I learned about a partially built home in Los Altos Hills. We purchased the house, hired a contractor to finish the building, and with plans drawn up by the celebrated landscape architect Thomas Church, I put in the trees, shrubs, and flower beds myself. By 1958 we moved again, to a house we built higher in the hills, surrounded by apricot orchards, where I still live.

Chapter 5

From Partnership to Corporation

IN 1947 WE incorporated Hewlett-Packard. This allowed for some tax advantages and also provided more continuity to the business than a partnership could. By that time we had also put in place a good part of the top-management team that was to guide the company over the next thirty years. Ed Porter had finally joined us, concentrating on the production end of things. Noel Eldred headed marketing and Frank Cavier, finance.

By 1950 our employment had gotten back up to its wartime peak of about two hundred. After having expanded into a Quonset hut, we built a more permanent plant adjacent to our existing facilities. We designed it to be a general-purpose building, and I remember thinking that if we couldn't keep the company going, we could lease out the building as a supermarket.

The company grew very rapidly in the early 1950s,

growth that was stimulated in part by the Korean War. But we had also built a good foundation on which to grow, and, thanks to some hard work we had undertaken in the late 1940s, our product line had grown to more than one hundred items by 1952. We also had improved and expanded our manufacturing operations to keep pace with the increasing number of products. And, under Noel Eldred, our network of sales representatives had become more efficient and productive. Between 1950 and 1951 our sales doubled and from 1951 to 1952 they doubled again.

After World War II Fred Terman had returned to Stanford from Harvard's Radio Research Laboratory. We resumed our close relationship with Fred, and together we developed a fellowship program whereby Stanford graduate engineering students would research and then design and build a product for HP. One of these graduate students, who had done his undergraduate work at Cal Tech, was Al Bagley. We wanted to develop a high-speed counter for measuring nuclear radioactivity, and Bagley was assigned to this project. It turned out he was able to develop an electronic counter that would operate at a frequency of up to ten megacycles. This took the counter beyond its original purpose and enabled us to make a frequency counter out of it and add it to the HP product line. This frequency counter was not very reliable and we assigned one of our engineers, Marv Wilrodt, to provide repair service at our customer's location. The counter was so useful when it did work that our customers tolerated its unreliability.

*Dave Packard, Bill Hewlett, and Fred Terman outside the
Stanford Electronic Research Laboratory in 1952. A gift from
Hewlett-Packard Company provided an additional wing to be used
as an instruction lab.*

This is a long way from what we have to do today in providing long-term reliability in our products. Starting with this single product, Al Bagley and his design team developed a growing family of frequency counters and related products that have been among the most successful of HP's offerings and that, over the years, have accounted for billions of dollars in sales.

Our collaboration with Stanford and Fred Terman continued, and in 1954 we expanded on the fellowship program and established what became known as the Honors Cooperative Program, which allowed qualified HP engineers to pursue advanced degrees at Stanford. The program made it possible for us to hire top-level young graduates from around the country with the promise that if they came to work for us and we thought it appropriate, they could attend graduate school while on full HP salary. Originally, the company paid part of their tuition as well, and more recently has paid all of their tuition. More than four hundred HP engineers have obtained master's or doctorate degrees through this program. It has enabled us to hire the top engineering graduates from universities all across the country for a number of years—an important factor in the ultimate success of our company.

In the early 1950s Stanford created the Stanford Industrial Park, a development that further strengthened its ties with local industry. The university, largely through the efforts once again of Fred Terman, set aside 579 acres of Stanford land adjacent to its Palo Alto campus to be developed into attractive sites for research laboratories, offices, and light-manufacturing facilities. Companies leased the land from Stanford and, under strict zoning ordinances and architectural controls, designed and constructed their own buildings.

In 1956 we began construction of our first two buildings in the park. Varian Associates had preceded us as a tenant, but over the years HP has become the largest tenant, with facilities totaling more than one million square feet.

The Stanford Park, the first of its kind in the nation, now has more than eighty tenants. Like Hewlett-Packard, many of these organizations have close ties with the university, especially with the engineering and business schools.

In 1952 I became a rancher for the first time. Bill and I had been deer hunting at a place named San Felipe just south of San Francisco Bay. We liked the area, so when the land was offered for sale we decided to begin a ranching partnership. It was a family participation arrangement from the first. Most of the Hewlett and Packard children learned to swim in the pool at San Felipe. The children rode horses through the hills and learned about the pleasures and problems of cattle raising. After a few years, we added to the original ranch with the purchase of Los Huecos, to the south of the original tract. Later, we bought ranch land in Idaho and also in the Central Valley of California. Several years ago, conservationists claimed we had damaged the range in Idaho by running too many head of cattle on it. As a matter of fact, due to steps Bill and I have taken to improve the land, game in that area now is five times what it was when we first acquired the land.

I have enjoyed many pleasures as the result of my experiences as a rancher; I've also learned a thing or two. Every season we would round up the cattle from the range and drive them to the corral. Along the way, we'd come to a gate; the trick was to get them through the gate and not stampede them. I found, after much trial and error, that applying steady gentle pressure from the rear worked best. Eventually, one would decide to pass through the gate; the rest would soon follow. Press them too hard, and they'd panic, scattering in all

Hunting at San Felipe ranch, 1970 (left to right): Ernie Arbuckle, Bill Hewlett, Noel Eldred, Maury Doyle, and Dave Packard.

directions. Slack off entirely, and they'd just head back to their old grazing spots. This insight was useful throughout my management career.

Another benefit from ranching was my friendship with Bill Hewlett. By running the ranches together—as well as the company—Bill and I developed a unique understanding of each other. This harmony has served us well every single day in running HP.

A Watershed Year

In many respects, 1957 was a watershed year for HP. At the end of 1956, new orders were at an all-time high. Our production had expanded tremendously, and we had increased our number of employees from 779 on January 1, 1956, to 1,268 on January 1, 1957. Our 395 Page Mill Road site included four buildings. And by September 1957, our first building (of six planned) in the Stanford Industrial Park was completed and in production. Our second building, a new laboratory, opened in October.

In November 1957, Hewlett-Packard stock was first offered to the public. Ten percent of the common stock Bill Hewlett and I owned became available at $16 per share. The 1957 offering, and later offerings, broadened the base of HP ownership and enabled our employees to become shareowners. It also facilitated our acquisition of other companies in the late 1950s and early 1960s.

Another 1957 event that had significance for the

company, especially for our business outside the United States, was the signing of the Treaty of Rome. Until then we had done relatively little to develop foreign markets for our products. For some years we had retained an export agent in San Francisco to sell HP products through a network of overseas sales representatives. This worked reasonably well, but by 1954 it was apparent that we needed to mount a more aggressive effort. So we created an export department that dealt directly with the overseas representatives.

When the Treaty of Rome was signed in 1957, HP exports accounted for 11 percent of our total sales. The importance of the treaty to companies like ours was that it led to the creation of the European Common Market, which in time became an immense market for electronic products. But it was a market favoring locally produced products as opposed to imports from the United States. Thus it became critical for U.S. companies to establish not only a marketing presence within the European market but a manufacturing presence as well.

Bill Hewlett was especially enthusiastic about the Common Market and thoroughly convinced of its promising business opportunities for HP. So, with the help of Bill Doolittle, Ray Demere, and attorney Nate Finch, he immediately began to investigate the pros and cons of setting up operations in various countries. After weighing his findings and narrowing the choices, he made trips to three countries and arranged meetings with bankers, local government officials, executives of manufacturing firms, and U.S. consulates.

In April 1959, we opened an office in Geneva, Switzerland, which became our European headquarters. In July, an HP sales operation got under way in West Germany. And in September we opened a small instrument-assembly plant in the town of Böblingen, near Stuttgart, West Germany. From that modest base we steadily expanded our European operations. In 1994 Europe accounted for more than one-third of HP's total business.

China

Hewlett-Packard now produces and sells thousands of products in more than 650 plants and offices located in over 120 countries around the world. As I have said many times, our success depends in large part on giving the responsibility to the level where it can be exercised effectively, usually on the lowest possible level of the organization, the level nearest the customer.

Hewlett-Packard's presence in the Far East goes back to the very early years of the company, and I will speak later of our long-standing business relationship with Japan and with Japanese enterprises.

I went to the People's Republic of China for the first time in November 1977, as part of the Committee on the Present Danger. This group was established because a number of people, myself included, felt we were not strengthening our military capability fast enough to counter the rapid buildup in the Soviet Union. We wanted the Committee on the Present Danger to be nonpartisan, which is why we delayed the formal announcement of its formation until after President Carter was inaugurated in 1977. Shortly afterward, the Chinese government invited us to visit them to discuss how we might help in dealing with the Soviet Union along China's northern border.

General Brent Scowcroft, Joe Fowler (the secretary of the treasury in the Johnson administration), Paul Nitze, Max Kampelman, and I went to China with our wives. Upon arriving, we were met by the foreign minister. The government had arranged an interesting trip for us, starting at Beijing and covering a wide span of the country. When we returned to Beijing at the end of our tour, the minister described how their government felt about each of the nations on their border. I remember that when he came to Hong Kong he said we should not worry about their relations there, for where else could they sell their snakes and turtles. A smaller number of us were invited for another visit in 1979.

Henry Kissinger had just visited China, and the Chinese had complained to him that they were not getting any help from the Carter administration. Dr. Kissinger suggested they invite some Americans from the private sector and he gave them my name, among others. Shortly thereafter, I received an invitation to visit and consult on industrial policy and military logistics.

I was tremendously excited by this invitation. Finally, I saw an opportunity for a substantive business conversation with the Chinese. In great haste, I assembled a special delegation: just myself, Lucile, and Chi-Ning Liu, an engineer at HP who was the son of a Nationalist Chinese general.

Our host was to be Ye Zhen-hua, vice chief of research and development for the Chinese army. Since I'd been to China before, I knew the activities in Beijing that I wanted to revisit. I gave my host a list of these, and we spent the first week visiting them. I did not have any idea about whether we were making any progress.

They gave us a free day on Sunday. When our host joined us on the following day, he said that Wang Zhen, a vice premier and survivor of the Long March, was holding a reception for us at the Great Hall of the People that afternoon, and he was also hosting a dinner for us at the same location. I immediately knew then that we *were* getting somewhere.

That evening, we laid our plan for the week: Lucile wanted to go to Xi'an to see the ceramic soldiers; unfortunately, we were told that Xi'an was closed. But the next day we were told, "We are going to Xi'an today."

While Lucile examined the ceramic soldiers, our hosts set up two very interesting visits for me in the area: one to a factory that was making anti-aircraft radar, using 1950s technology, about which I knew a great deal. They allowed me to examine the equipment in a field behind the plant where they were conducting tests. There were about 4,000 people at this facility, and we were the first Americans ever to visit. It was obvious to me that what they were building would be entirely useless in modern-day combat, but I didn't say anything at the time, except to compliment them on their workmanship.

The next day we visited a plant making turbine engines, again using 1950s Soviet technology. They had a test facility there for measuring the efficiency of the engines: thrust, fuel consumption, that sort of thing.

I tried to commend their work once more, though again their equipment was easily twenty-five years out of date. And I told my guides that I would happily arrange some meetings in the United States so that they could learn about our work in related fields.

Then we had dinner with Chi-Ning Liu's family, including his brother and his brother's wife. His brother had served in the Korean War, fighting against the United States. Afterward, he settled in Xi'an and became a teacher. They had three daughters. The oldest was an excellent violin player, and the youngest was the local Ping-Pong champion. At this dinner, they put on a Ping-Pong contest for us to watch, and we had an interesting time discussing what had happened in China since Chi-Ning Liu had emigrated in July 1949.

We returned to Beijing, and a couple of days before we left they said they wanted to form a joint venture with Hewlett-Packard. I said that was OK, but I wanted to know what the rules were going to be. They said that I could make the rules. They set up a special corporate entity to deal with us and sent a dozen engineers and managers to the United States to see how we conducted our business. My host in China came to the United

States the following year while the dozen Chinese engineers and managers were visiting our Palo Alto facility. Together, they visited our ranch in Merced. At the time we were having a roundup; he and his people watched cattle branding and sampled some Rocky Mountain oysters. Lu and I invited them to our place in Big Sur near Monterey. As hosts, we got there ahead of our guests and realized that we didn't have any chopsticks in the house. So I went out into the shop and made a dozen sets of chopsticks out of redwood. When our guests arrived, they asked me to autograph their new handmade chopsticks, which I did. And they took them back to China as souvenirs.

In 1983 they invited us to bring the entire HP board of directors to China for a meeting. Our company has enjoyed an extraordinary relationship with China ever since. For their part, the Chinese have been able to acquire from us the instrumentation they need to build up their fledgling electronics-manufacturing capability. Our business is very active in China: We have several manufacturing plants, and we sell HP products mainly in the industrial area along the east coast of the Chinese mainland.

More Structure

Our rapid growth up to 1956 had brought to light some organizational weaknesses. And with prospects for continuing growth ahead, I thought it was time to

HP's full product line in 1959 — 380 products.

provide more structure to the company and a better
delineation of goals and responsibilities. By 1957 our
product line included more than three hundred instruments, our annual sales were approaching $30 million,
and we had ninety engineers engaged in product development. It was time to organize these engineers into
smaller, more efficient groups, which we did by form-
ing four product-development groups. Each group concentrated on a family of related products, and each had
a senior engineering head reporting to Dr. Bernard
Oliver. That was Barney Oliver, our old friend from
Stanford whom we managed to entice from Bell Laboratories in 1952. We appointed him vice president of
research and development.

One of the new divisions concentrated on frequency
counters and related instruments, another on microwave equipment, a third on audio and video products,
and the fourth on oscilloscopes.

There is an interesting story behind our work in oscilloscopes. During the war Bill Hewlett had gotten to know a bright young engineer named Howard Vollum. He was impressed with Vollum, so much so that he urged me to talk with him. This was while Bill was still in the army. I arranged for Vollum to visit us, and he and I had a long chat. He told me he was keenly interested in designing a new type of oscilloscope, which is a fundamental measuring instrument. He wanted to design one with a triggered sweep, a concept from radar technology.

During our conversation it became clear to both of us that rather than joining HP, Vollum really wanted to start his own company . . . and we helped him do just that. We lined him up with Norm Neely and many of our other sales representative firms across the United States. Thus was born Tektronix, the Oregon-based company that became the dominant oscilloscope supplier in the world.

As time went on it became quite clear that if we were going to offer a complete line of electronic measuring instruments, we needed to fill in the line with our own oscilloscope. So in 1956 we designed an oscilloscope, the Model 150, which we hoped would provide a strong challenge to Tektronix. But as it turned out, the 150 was very unreliable, and of course we had to do our best to improve it. In retrospect we should have gotten into the oscilloscope business much earlier than we did. But even after we had built up a family of well-designed, high-quality oscilloscopes, Tektronix had such a strong position that over the next few years we were able to capture only about 15 percent of the market. We developed an oscilloscope system managed by a computer some years later, and we were able to dominate the market with that system.

Getting back to the restructuring of our product-development staff, there was another important reason why we split it into divisions. This allowed a design engineer to concentrate only on the division's products and to work closely with the appropriate field salespeople to get a good fix on customer needs and opinions.

Meeting in Sonoma

Another significant event that occurred early in 1957 was the company's first off-site meeting of senior managers. This was a two-day meeting that took place at the Sonoma Mission Inn, about seventy miles north of San Francisco. About twenty people attended.

Bill Hewlett and I decided to have the meeting for at least three reasons. First, we thought it a good idea to get our key managers together at least once a year to discuss policies and problems, to exchange views, and to make plans for the future. Second, there were now more than 1,200 people in the company, making it increasingly difficult for Bill and me to know everyone well and to have a personal knowledge of everything that was going on. So we felt it essential that despite HP's growth, we try to maintain a small-company atmosphere and to have our key managers thoroughly familiar with our mangement style and objectives.

The third reason we had the meeting was to present to the group for their review and study a set of corporate objectives that I had previously drafted and discussed with Bill. By way of background, Bill and I often thought about how a company like ours should be organized and managed. We thought that if we could get everybody to agree on what our objectives were and to understand what we were trying to do, then we could turn them loose and they would move in a common direction.

We devoted a good part of the Sonoma meeting to a review and discussion of the proposed objectives. Bill and I felt strongly that if our managers and supervisors were to be guided by written objectives, they should have a part in developing them. We also pointed out that objectives were meant to be evaluated from time to time and, if necessary, to be modified for the future benefit of the company.

There were six original objectives. As time went on we refined these objectives, based on our experience with them and on changes in the business environment. We published a second version of the objectives in 1966 and they were as follows:

1. *Profit.* To recognize that profit is the best single measure of our contribution to society and the ultimate source of our corporate strength. We should

attempt to achieve the maximum possible profit consistent with our other objectives.

2. *Customers.* To strive for continual improvement in the quality, usefulness, and value of the products and services we offer our customers.

3. *Field of Interest.* To concentrate our efforts, continually seeking new opportunities for growth but limiting our involvement to fields in which we have capability and can make a contribution.

4. *Growth.* To emphasize growth as a measure of strength and a requirement for survival.

5. *Employees.* To provide employment opportunities for HP people that include the opportunity to share in the company's success, which they help make possible. To provide for them job security based on performance, and to provide the opportunity for personal satisfaction that comes from a sense of accomplishment in their work.

6. *Organization.* To maintain an organizational environment that fosters individual motivation, initiative and creativity, and a wide latitude of freedom in working toward established objectives and goals.

7. *Citizenship.* To meet the obligations of good citizenship by making contributions to the community and to the institutions in our society which generate the environment in which we operate.

Each of these objectives was supported by text that explained why it was chosen and that discussed in some detail the evolution and importance of the objective. Though the full texts are not repeated here, I will be referring to them when I talk, in the following pages, about the objectives in the broader context of what has come to be called the HP Way.

Any organization, any group of people who have worked together for some time, develops a philosophy, a set of values, a series of traditions and customs. These, in total, are unique to the organization. So it is with Hewlett-Packard. We have a set of values—deeply held beliefs that guide us in meeting our objectives, in working with one another, and in dealing with customers, shareholders, and others. Our corporate objectives are built upon these values. The objectives serve as a day-to-day guide for decision making. To help us meet our objectives, we employ various plans and practices. It is the combination of these elements—our values, corporate objectives, plans and practices—that forms the HP Way and that is the subject of the chapters that follow.

Chapter 6

Growth from Profit

AT HEWLETT-PACKARD (and other companies as well), people, materials, facilities, money, and time are the resources available to us for conducting our business. By applying our skills, we turn these resources into useful products and services. If we do a good job, customers pay us more for our products than the sum of our costs in producing and distributing them. This difference, our profit, represents the value we add to the resources we utilize.

It is impossible to operate a business for long unless it generates a profit, and so if a company is to meet any of its other objectives, it must make a profit. Our ability to properly serve our customers, to finance research and development, to offer rewarding employment opportunities, and to make contributions to the communities in which we operate all depend directly on our ability to generate an adequate profit. The profit we generate from our operations is the ultimate source of the funds we need to prosper and grow. It's the foundation of future opportunity and employment security.

The profit that can reasonably be expected on each product varies with its competitive situation, the unique value of that product, and the capital investment necessary to produce it. Therefore, the same profit level cannot be expected from each product or from each division or unit of the company.

Sixty years ago our country was in the depths of the Great Depression. Thousands of businesses had shut their doors, and one of every three people in the labor force was out of work. Bill Hewlett and I were raised during that depression. We had observed its devastating effects on people, including many families and friends who were close to us.

My father had been appointed as a bankruptcy referee for the state of Colorado. When I returned to Pueblo during the summers of the 1930s, I often helped my father in looking up the records of those companies that had gone bankrupt. I noted that the banks simply foreclosed on firms that mortgaged their assets and these firms were left with nothing. Those firms that did not borrow money had a difficult time, but they ended up with their assets intact and survived during the depression years that followed.

From this experience I decided our company should not incur any long-term debt. For this reason Bill and I determined we would operate the company on a pay-as-you-go basis, financing our growth primarily out of earnings rather than by borrowing money. We knew self-financing was possible because General Radio, a company we admired, had been in business several years, had been successful, and had never sought outside financing. Our feeling was if they could do it, we could do it. And we have—for more than a half century.

I know that in some industries, particularly those requiring large capital investments, the pay-as-you-go approach just isn't feasible. I also know that it has become popular throughout industry to meet capital needs by leveraging profits with equity financing and long-term borrowing. The advocates of this approach say you can make your profits go further by leveraging them. That may be, but at HP it was our firm policy to pay as we go and not to incur substantial debt.

Our long-standing policy has been to reinvest most of our profits and to depend on this reinvestment, plus funds from employee stock purchases and other cash flow items, to finance our growth. The stock purchase plan allows employees to apply up to a certain percentage of their salaries to purchase shares of HP stock at a preferential price. The company picks up a portion of the price of the stock. The plan has been in existence since 1959 and has provided us with significant amounts of cash to help finance our growth.

In setting up the stock purchase plan we made one important mistake. We did not require our employees who bought HP stock at a preferential price to keep it. There is a long-standing truth about wage and salary levels—no matter what the pay, the employee thinks he or she needs about 10 percent more. We found that many of our people who participated in this preferential stock purchase plan sold their stock right away. Even our employees at high levels had standing orders to sell their stock as soon as they received it.

That situation has been corrected, but it is ironic that many of our employees who held on to their stock and sold it when they retired often had gains of more than a million dollars.

A Critical Test

Our policy of self-financing requires not only a reasonable level of profit but also good management of assets. This policy underwent a critical test in the early 1970s. Following a period of worldwide recession and slow growth, the company faced a rebounding market. With limited cash to work with, it was giving serious consideration to some long-term borrowing, as much as $100 million. We had priced some of our products too low, our inventories and accounts receivable were at alarmingly high levels, and we were doing a poor job of controlling costs. But I was convinced we could correct the problem through greater self-discipline. I quickly visited nearly every one of our major divisions, meeting with a host of managers and giving them a lecture that was later characterized by one manager as "Dave's give-'em-hell talk." The response was impressive. Our managers really knuckled down . . . inventories were sharply reduced, accounts receivable were tightened, costs came under better control. We got the whole team working on the problem, and the company went on to experience a period of strong, profitable growth without resorting to long-term borrowing.

In analyzing our accounts receivable we found a major weakness. Many of our customers were buying products from several HP entities to combine into a system. They were not paying for any of the products until they received the last one needed.

We changed this procedure so that we were able to put the system together and check it out before it was delivered. This provided an incentive to HP entities to expedite production of products. It assured that the system worked properly, and it helped solve the accounts receivable problem.

A positive fallout from this entire episode was the clear reminder that self-financing requires constant vigilance and self-discipline.

Responsibility to Shareholders

An important element of the HP Way has to do with the company's relationship with its shareholders and the investment community. A primary objective in this area is to provide consistency in our corporate performance, including steady growth in earnings and equity. Obviously, this is not always possible, even for the best of corporations, but over the years our Hewlett-Packard performance has been quite good.

HP common stock first came into being in 1947, when we transformed our original partnership into a corporation. Ten years later, to broaden the base of ownership, Bill and I offered, for public sale, 10 percent of the 3 million shares outstanding. Also in 1957 the company distributed 60,000 new shares to employees as bonuses, as well as making available another 50,000 shares for employee stock options. At that time public trading began in the over-the-counter market.

In 1959 we initiated our employee stock purchase plan. Employee participation has been active, and the basic plan remains in effect today. In 1961 HP stock was accepted simultaneously for listing on the New

HP lists on the New York Stock Exchange, March 17, 1961 (left to right): Dave Packard; Keith Funston, president of the NYSE; and Mortimer Marcus, specialist in the stock.

York and Pacific Stock Exchanges, and in recent years it has been listed on the principal foreign exchanges as well.

We had two main purposes in going public with our stock in 1957. One was to broaden the ownership of the company, especially employee ownership. The other was to have stock available in the event we wanted to acquire other companies. It is often more practical to acquire a company by an exchange of stock than by outright purchase. As it turned out, we acquired several companies in the 1960s, most of them through an exchange of stock.

The day of our first public listing on the New York Stock Exchange did not start smoothly. A few of us flew to New York the day before the event and stayed uptown at the Essex House. Early the next morning, we set off for Wall Street. It never occurred to me to take a taxi; instead, we jumped on the BMT subway and headed downtown. Unfortunately, I wasn't much of a subway navigator; after much debate, we made the wrong connection at Times Square. We arrived on Wall Street several minutes late and were immediately ushered into a huge corner office and greeted by the chairman of the exchange, Keith Funston. He chuckled when I explained that we'd gotten lost on the subway. I don't think he could fathom that we would take the subway to such an important event. But we did!

Over the years our communications with shareholders and the investment community have, I believe, reflected our basic philosophies and the HP Way. We have endeavored to be forthright and candid, and have practiced full and prompt disclosure of events or developments having a real or potential effect on the price of Hewlett-Packard stock.

Wall Street's Short-Term Focus

Much has been said and written about Wall Street's seeming fixation on quarterly earnings. And indeed, the focus on short-term results often has a significant effect on the price of a company's stock. Moreover, that effect is frequently unrelated to the basic strength and long-term prospects of the company.

It is always possible to improve profits for a time by reducing the level of our investment in new-product design and engineering, in customer service, or in new buildings and equipment. But in the long run we will pay a severe price for overlooking any of these areas. One of our most important management tasks is maintaining the proper balance between short-term profit performance and investment for future strength and growth.

Good new products are the lifeblood of technical companies such as ours, although our business levels vary from year to year. A strong research and development effort has always been the driving force behind product contribution at HP. Over the years our annual expenditures on R&D have amounted to between 8 and 10 percent of sales, and in recent years have exceeded 10 percent. In meeting our profit objective we are always mindful at HP of the long pull—steadily adding strength and value to the company.

The pricing of new products is an important and challenging exercise. Often a product will be introduced to the market at a price too low to make an adequate short-term profit. The thinking is that "we'll get our costs down and that will enable us to make a good profit"— either next month, next quarter, or next year. But that time seldom, if ever, comes.

Often pricing also falls prey to the goal of "market share." Many managers in American industry are caught up with the idea of capturing a larger share of a market, often by undercutting the competition's prices. In the short term, that often results in an impressive sales volume . . . but at the expense of little or no profit.

In 1972 we introduced a product that redefined the calculator market. It was the Model 35 handheld calculator, the world's first "electronic slide rule." We priced the product at $395, which was considered high by many and excessive by some. But the calculator represented such a unique *value* that once it hit the market, we couldn't make them fast enough. Not too many months later we had aggressive competitors, companies that offered calculators at prices substantially below HP's. Their goal, which they readily admitted, was to capture market share from us . . . and they did. But in the long term we made a profit by making sure we kept our costs down.

At that time our policy at HP was to regard increased

market share as a reward for doing things well—for providing customers with superior products and services and keeping our costs down. This has been a basic policy from the very beginning of our company, and we expect it to continue in the future.

Chapter 7

Commitment
to Innovation

WHEN BILL HEWLETT AND I put together the
initial plans for our business enterprise in 1937, we
hadn't yet focused our interest and energies on the field
of electronic instrumentation. What we did decide,
however, was that we wanted to direct our efforts
toward making important technical contributions to
the advancement of science, industry, and human welfare. It was a lofty, ambitious goal. But right from the
beginning, Bill and I knew we didn't want to be a "me-
too" company merely copying products already on the
market. To this day, HP continually strives to develop
products that represent true advancement.

The original Hewlett-Packard products were electronic measuring instruments. With growth, our product line expanded and so, too, did our field of interest.
In the period after World War II, we put a great deal of
effort into designing better instruments. We had come

to realize that a successful new instrument had to include new technology and be useful. This meant that the most important new instruments would combine new technology and demonstrate marketability. There were, from time to time, new development opportunities that included new technology in areas where we had no marketing capability. These we sold to firms that had the marketing ability.

We started a monthly publication in 1949 called the *HP Journal*. It was patterned after a journal of the General Radio Company called the *Experimentor*. The *HP Journal* described the technology used in the development of important new products. Although this information was useful to our competitors, we thought the benefits outweighed this disadvantage. The *Journal* was published monthly, and often there were several issues describing a new development and its application. I will not cover every development we made but I will describe some of the important ones.

We were involved with quartz frequency standards for a long time. In the course of this work we learned about a scientist in Colorado, Don Hammond, who was doing some excellent work with quartz. We asked him to join our company. He developed a number of new kinds of instruments for us using quartz. One was a quartz thermometer that could measure temperature with a resolution of .0001 degrees C. It can be located some distance from the digital readout without any loss of accuracy and it can do a number of things no other thermometer can do.

Our laser interferometer was another real break-through in technology. It uses a two-frequency laser and can make measurements that are accurate to a millionth of an inch. It is ideal for measuring machine tool accuracy and it can be used to measure distances of two hundred feet. A large number of our engineers participated in this project. Len Cutler and Al Bagley took the lead. Joe Rando, John Dukes, Gary Gordon, Andre Rude, Kenneth Wayne, Richard Baldwin, Glenn Brugwald, William Kruger, and many others worked on it. The project was described in the *Journal* in August 1970. HP has been number one in the world market ever since.

One of our most important contributions related to light emitting diodes. More than six years of research and development on light emitting materials was involved. Our work in other areas, such as solid state technology and integrated circuit technology, also contributed. We had LED work to the point where it could have been used in the early 1960s, but none of our divisions chose to use it. Despite that fact, Bill Hewlett and I decided we should keep this work going. It made the pocket-sized calculator possible in 1972 and it has become the display in many applications since. Howard Borden and Gerald Pighini described this development in the *HP Journal* in the late 1960s. LED applications have expanded far beyond what was envisioned at that time. We have continued the development of light emitting materials, and our latest contribution is the brightest light emitting diodes in the world. These will find wide use in automobile taillights and turn signal lights. The first automobile to use them is the 1995 Thunderbird. They have a great advantage over incandescent lights. They never burn out and they use much less energy. They will increase the mileage of an automobile by one mile per gallon and thus pay for themselves very quickly. It should be only a short time before all of the automobiles in the world will be equipped with these light emitting diodes.

The key to HP's prospective involvement in any field of interest is *contribution*. Our objective is to expand and diversify only when we can build on our present strengths, and with the recognition that we have the proven capability to make a contribution. To meet this objective, it is important that we put maximum effort into our product-development programs. This means we must continually seek new ideas for new and better kinds of products.

A constant flow of good new products is the lifeblood of Hewlett-Packard and essential to our growth. Early on we developed a system for measuring the flow and success of new products. This system is represented in five-year Vintage Charts (see Appendix 3).

In the 1970s and early 1980s, as more of our products involved computers, our vintage charts show that our existing computers continued to sell well long after they were introduced because new developments largely involved software. New software gave our computer systems a lifetime of several decades. This meant HP customers could rely on their computers for a long period.

And it helped our distributed systems gain a foothold in a market that had been dominated by the mainframe computers of IBM and DEC.

At HP, as in other technical companies, there is no shortage of ideas. The problem is to select those likely to fill a *real need* in the marketplace.

To warrant serious pursuit an idea must be both practical (the device under consideration must work properly) and useful. Out of those ideas that are practical, a smaller number are useful. To be useful an invention must not only fill a need, it must be an economical and efficient solution to that need.

When HP was making primarily test and measuring instruments for engineers, we had a built-in method for helping us determine what customers might need in the way of innovative new instruments. We called it the "next bench" syndrome. If the idea for a new instrument appealed to the HP engineer working at the next bench, it would very likely appeal to our customers as well. As our business expanded, input from our non-engineer customers was a critical factor in helping us decide what kinds of product ideas to pursue. We always asked, "How can we make a contribution based on our strengths and our knowledge?" Then we'd ask, "Who needs it?"

No company has unlimited resources, so it is essential that the resources available be applied to the projects most likely to be successful. At HP we often used to select projects on the basis of a six-to-one engineering return. That is, the profit we expected to derive over the lifetime of a product should be at least six times greater than the cost of developing the product. Almost without exception, the products that beat the six-to-one ratio by the widest margin were the most innovative.

The Institute of Radio Engineers (IRE) was the professional society for people engaged in radio engineering. Each spring the society met in New York City. Accompanying the meeting was an exhibit of radio equipment from various manufacturers. I attended my first IRE show in New York in the spring of 1940. I kept the cost down by staying with friends. The equipment display that year was in the ballroom of the Commodore Hotel. I had a table about four feet by eight feet on which to show our Hewlett-Packard instruments. From that beginning in 1940, the IRE show and convention grew rapidly, and I attended every year until 1969, when I took the job as U.S. deputy secretary of defense. Some years before that, the membership of the IRE had been expanded, and the society became the Institute of Electrical and Electronics Engineers, commonly known as the IEEE.

In the early days we went to the New York show and convention by train. We took the train leaving San Francisco Friday afternoon, arriving in Chicago Sunday morning. That afternoon we took another train out of Chicago, arriving Monday morning in New York. On our way back we often spent a day or two in Chicago. Our sales representative in Chicago was a fine gentleman named Al Crossley. I was always amused by our visits with him because everything he pointed out to us in Chicago was the "biggest in the world."

The New York show lasted three or four days, during which exhibitors tried to attract large numbers of customers and prospects to whom they could demonstrate their new products. We also made a point of checking out our competitors' products. The days were long, and after dinner we often relaxed by going down to Greenwich Village to listen to some Dixieland music.

As time went on the show increased in size and importance, attracting thousands of visitors. It also

HP shows off its first computer in 1967 at the IEEE trade show in New York City.

became a focal point for our product-development efforts. Each year there was mounting pressure to have products "ready for IRE," and sometimes we'd take instruments to New York that weren't completely checked out. In that case we'd hole up in our hotel rooms, sometimes for an entire evening, to make sure the instruments would work properly at the show the next day.

Lab managers face a real challenge in dealing with the enthusiastic inventor who presents a very creative and innovative idea—an idea that after careful and objective analysis by others is turned down. How do managers provide encouragement and help the inventor retain enthusiasm in the face of such disappointment?

Many HP managers over the years have expressed admiration for the way Bill Hewlett handled these situations. One manager has called it Bill's "hat-wearing process." Upon first being approached by a creative inventor with unbridled enthusiasm for a new idea, Bill immediately put on a hat called "enthusiasm." He would listen, express excitement where appropriate and appreciation in general, while asking a few rather gentle and not too pointed questions. A few days later, he would get back to the inventor wearing a hat called "inquisition." This was the time for very pointed questions, a thorough probing of the idea, lots of give-and-take. Without a final decision, the session was adjourned. Shortly thereafter, Bill would put on his "decision" hat and meet once again with the inventor. With appropriate logic and sensitivity, judgment was rendered and a decision made about the idea. This process provided the inventor with a sense of satisfaction, even when the decision went against the project— a vitally important outcome for engendering continued enthusiasm and creativity.

Entry into the Computer Age

In 1994, HP's sales in computer products, service, and support were almost $20 billion, or about 78 percent of the company's total business. In 1964, our sales totaled $125 million and were entirely in instruments. Not a penny was from computer sales.

This represents a remarkable transformation of our company and its business. It would be nice to claim that we foresaw the profound effect of computers on our business and that we prepared ourselves to take early advantage of the computer age. Unfortunately, the record does not justify such pride. It would be more accurate to say that we were pushed into computers by the revolution that was changing electronics.

In the early 1960s it became apparent that computers could play a major role in the instrument field. It was recognized that a computer could improve the accuracy of an electronic instrument tenfold or more, as well as make the output more useful.

I took a trip to New England to investigate several small computer companies. It was clear to me that the Digital Equipment Company (DEC) had some promising products. I visited them and discussed the possibility of their joining us. It appeared that we might be able to acquire DEC for about $25 million. But there were some complicating factors and we decided not to pursue the matter further. I also visited Wang Laboratories, which was designing an electronic calculator, but I decided at the time it would not be desirable for us to get involved in electronic calculators.

Meanwhile two of our engineers, Kay Magleby and Paul Stoft, began to experiment with building a computer. They presented me with a vision of a system of HP computers automating HP instruments that were connected to our printers and plotters. I began to get excited about the prospect of an HP computer.

In September 1964, we began to develop an automatic controller for measurement systems with Kay Magleby heading the team. This was to become our first minicomputer, the Model 2116. Although the work had started in our Hewlett-Packard Laboratories, we acquired a small computer group from Union Carbide to help staff the effort. This was the nucleus of our early computer division in Cupertino, not far from Palo Alto.

We soon found that we were selling more 2116s as stand-alone minicomputers than as controllers in automatic measurement systems. Still, we were slow to get the message. An example of our cautious approach to computers was the way we handled a promising project, code-named Omega. Initiated by our people in Cupertino, Omega was what would have been, in the early 1970s, the world's first thirty-two-bit computer. The term thirty-two-bit refers to the word length used in the computer data format and to the width of the parallel buses used to transport data in the machine. Initially, a word length of eight bits was common. In 1968, the standard had become sixteen bits. A thirty-two-bit machine would require more hardware but would have been twice as fast and would directly access thousands of times more memory.

The prospect of producing such a fast and powerful computer had created tremendous enthusiasm among our Cupertino people, and they soon had Omega at the prototype stage. By that time, however, there had been increasing top-management concern about the scope of the project. It clearly represented a departure from HP's basic principles. It was expensive. We would have to take on debt to fund it, and rather than building on existing HP strengths, the project required expertise and capabilities we did not have at the time, such as an electronic data-processing center, large-business processing applications, twenty-four-hour service, plus leasing and sales operations. More important was the fact that the thirty-two-bit computer project presented a new and formidable marketing challenge. It would take us into unfamiliar commercial markets and into direct competition with IBM's mainframe business. Bill Hewlett's sage advice had always been, "Don't try to take a fortified hill, especially if the army on top is bigger than your own." Omega was a case in point. The project was canceled, a decision that was difficult and controversial.

The cancellation of Omega was especially disappointing to our Cupertino people. The fellow who had been running the project left the division (and, soon afterward, the company). Several people who remained took to wearing black-velvet armbands, in mourning for the canceled project. Canceled it may have been . . . but not abandoned! It turned out that a few of the Omega enthusiasts kept the project hidden in a back room of the lab and were still working on it.

At that point several key managers and engineers took another look at the project. They concluded that it embodied some good ideas in terms of computer architecture and, if we could scale it back to a sixteen-bit machine and simplify the operating system, we might have a promising product. So the Omega development program was redirected and renamed "Alpha." The result was a sophisticated, low-cost, sixteen-bit machine for processing small to medium-sized on-line business transactions. Alpha became HP's first general-purpose computer, introduced in 1972 as the HP3000. The HP3000, with its MPE operating system, is one of the computer industry's most enduring success stories. More than twenty years after its introduction, its descendant machines are just now entering their obsolescent phase.

Electronic Calculators:
A Bright New Market

At the time of my visit to Wang, I didn't think HP should get into the calculator business. All this changed, however, when a young engineer named Tom Osborne paid a visit to HP in 1966. Tom had worked across the San Francisco Bay at Smith Corona Marchant, a supplier of mechanical calculators. He had built a model of a typewriter-size electronic calculator and had been trying to sell his concept, unsuccessfully, to various companies. At HP he showed his model to Paul Stoft, a senior HP Labs manager, and to Barney Oliver. They, and later Bill Hewlett and I, recognized that Osborne had a little powerhouse of a machine that perhaps could be developed into a desktop calculator capable of silently and swiftly calculating trigonometric, hyperbolic, and logarithmic functions—and be programmable as well. It would make obsolete the noisy mechanical calculators and the cumbersome tables of functions that crammed the engineer's bookshelf.

Working with Tom Osborne, an HP team developed the Model 9100 desktop calculator, highly successful in the marketplace and exemplifying truly innovative design. It was developed before the days of large-scale integrated circuits, so it included a fourteen-layer printed circuit board, the most demanding our shop had ever produced. Among the admirers of the 9100 was Arthur C. Clarke, the science fiction writer and author of *2001: A Space Odyssey*. His fans at HP discovered that he wanted a 9100 for Christmas and took up a collection to buy him one. He promptly named it HAL Junior after the computer in his movie, and said it was almost exactly the calculator he had drawn on his doodle pad one day when dreaming about what an engineer would really like. I took a 9100 with me to Washington when I joined the Defense Department in 1969.

Although the 9100 was immensely successful, the most exciting part of HP's calculator activity was still to come. As larger, lower-power integrated-circuit memories and IC processors became available, many of the engineers who had built the 9100 were eager to compress its functionality into a handheld device and meet Bill Hewlett's challenge of developing a calculator that could fit into a shirt pocket.

The calculator, called the HP 35 because it had thirty-five keys, was introduced in 1972. About a month before its release, Barney Oliver gave samples of the 35 to several leading engineers and Nobel physicists. The crowds they drew when casually showing off this "toy" at meetings and conventions probably accounted for our being unable to meet the initial demands for the 35 and later the programmable HP 65. Sales for these calculators and their descendants have now totaled over 15 million units. The log-log-trig slide rule, once the engineer's faithful friend, disappeared overnight.

With each product, HP strives, as I have said, to

make a contribution to the art—to add something new and different. Oddly enough, this desire, which helped us in the calculator and later in the computer field with our reduced instruction set computers (RISC), was actually a hindrance in entering the personal computer field. Much of the contribution in scientific and business computers is in honing the algorithms and matching the hardware to them to speed the operation. Initially, the hardware supplier furnished much of the software needed by the system. But over the years, many companies have arisen whose entire business is software. This is especially true for the personal computer (PC), whose owners couldn't care less about writing programs.

Today, if you do not offer PCs with a standard interface to the software suppliers whose products the user will buy, you will miss a large share of the market. We have had to learn that in today's computer world, the contribution we can make is in ease of use, speed, reliability, and above all, affordability.

A Maverick's Persistence

Earlier I mentioned that sometimes management's turndown of a new idea doesn't always effectively kill it. Some years ago, at an HP laboratory in Colorado Springs devoted to oscilloscope technology, one of our bright, energetic engineers, Chuck House, was advised to abandon a display monitor he was developing.

Instead, he embarked on a vacation to California—
stopping along the way to show potential customers a
prototype model of the monitor. He wanted to find out
what they thought, specifically what they wanted the
product to do and what its limitations were. Their positive reaction spurred him to continue with the project
even though, on his return to Colorado, he found that I,
among others, had requested it be discontinued. He
persuaded his R&D manager to rush the monitor into
production, and as it turned out, HP sold more than
seventeen thousand display monitors representing sales
revenue of $35 million for the company.

Several years later, at a gathering of HP engineers, I
presented Chuck with a medal for "extraordinary con-
tempt and defiance beyond the normal call of engineering duty."

So how does a company distinguish between insub-
ordination and entrepreneurship? To this young engineer's mind the difference lay in the intent.

"I wasn't trying to be defiant or obstreperous. I really
just wanted a success for HP," Chuck said. "It never
occurred to me that it might cost me my job." As a
postscript to the story, this same engineer later became
director of a department . . . with his reputation as a
maverick intact.

When one thinks of HP contributions, one usually
thinks of innovative products. But it's important to
point out that over the years we have attempted to
make contributions as well in the form of new manufacturing methods and techniques. These manufacturing

innovations often make state-of-the-art product contributions possible.

In many cases the development of new or improved production processes reflected a "can-do" attitude on the part of our manufacturing crews, a spirit and desire to find a better way of doing things. Both Bill and I encouraged it.

The Kingman card was one example. In about 1945, before the idea of printed circuitry came along, we used a technique developed by Rufe Kingman that greatly cut production costs and improved the reliability and serviceability of our products. The Kingman card was a strip with lugs on each side into which components were easily inserted and then soldered. It provided uniformity and allowed us to produce a standard component board.

Another example was the in-house integrated-circuit operation HP developed in the mid-1960s, long before any of our competitors. This capability anticipated the increased use of digital circuitry instrumentation. The IIP team developed not only their own bipolar process but also other equipment necessary for the production and testing of ICs before such equipment was available from outside vendors.

Our dedication to making a contribution, coupled with our commitment to understanding the potential needs of customers, served us well in allowing HP to adapt to both changing technologies and changing customer needs.

Chapter 8

Listening to Customers

THE FUNDAMENTAL BASIS for success in the operation of Hewlett-Packard is the job we do in satisfying the needs of our customers. We encourage every person in our organization to think continually about how his or her activities relate to the central purpose of serving our customers.

At HP, the customer satisfaction concept begins with the generation of new ideas and new technology from which we can develop useful, significant products. These new ideas then form the basis for development of products that will meet latent needs of future importance to our customers. To be useful in an era of worldwide competition and rapid change, new products must be developed quickly and produced efficiently with manufacturing processes and techniques that assure quality and economy.

Providing innovative, reliable products is a key element in satisfying customer needs, but there are other important elements as well. At HP we offer many different products to many different customers, and it's imperative that the products recommended to a specific customer are those that will best fulfill the customer's overall, long-term needs. This requires that our field salespeople—operating individually, in teams, or with other companies that add value to HP products and services—work closely with customers to determine the most appropriate, effective solutions to their problems.

When a customer buys a product from HP, the customer should expect not only that the product performs well the day it's received but that it be backed with the best possible service so that the customer can obtain long, trouble-free operation.

For many years HP's marketing and sales activities were headed by Noel Eldred, vice president of marketing. Noel, a key member of our top-management team, was a strong advocate for helping the customer, so much so that he wanted our sales engineers to take the customer's side in any disputes with the company. "We don't want you blindly agreeing with us," he'd tell them. "We want you to stick up for the customer. After all, we're not selling hardware; we're selling solutions to customer problems." Noel stressed the importance of customer feedback in helping us design and develop products aimed at real customer needs. He also insisted that our salespeople never speak disparagingly of the competition. This reflected our feeling that competitors should be respected, the type of respect that existed between General Radio and HP when Bill and I were starting out.

Earlier I talked about the HP 35 handheld calculator. The creation of this unique product presented tremendous challenges to its designers and its manufacturing team. Not only that, if we were to market the 35 successfully, we would have to develop methods of selling and distribution that were completely new to HP. Our traditional system of delivery—customers sent in orders and we shipped out products—clearly wouldn't work. So we sent some of our people to the Stanford University Bookstore and other retail outlets to see what we could do. One of our engineers, Bill Terry, vividly recalls going to Macy's department store in San Francisco. Macy's, at that time, was interested in building an electronics department. Bill remembers showing the calculator, eliciting interest, striking a deal on the price, and then starting to talk about order and delivery schedules. At that point the Macy's manager placed both hands squarely on the table in front of him, looked Bill in the eye, and said, "You young boys don't understand. I don't sell anything unless I have it in the store." That was our initiation into the consumer market.

Building to fill shelves was a new concept to HP. But our basic management principles translated easily to the high-volume retail business, and our decentralized business teams enabled us to be nimble enough to change business models quickly.

Our activity in the consumer market consisted of very little until the 1980s, although shortly after the introduction of the HP 35 we did try our hand at a calculator wristwatch. But the 01, as it was called, code-named Cricket, was clumsy and cumbersome—long on technology and short on fashion. We probably sold fewer than twenty thousand of them, mostly to our friends in the electronics industry. (Editor's note: In today's growing market for antique electronic gear, the HP 01 is quite sought after, often fetching more than twice its original price of $700.)

The Story of HP Printers

In 1994, Hewlett-Packard sold 5 million DeskJet printers and almost 4 million LaserJets. In the decade since these printers were introduced in 1984, our company has shipped 30 million printers. This extraordinary success can be traced back to the roots of our printer business in the early 1970s.

When HP entered the computer systems business in the late 1960s, we realized that computers and peripherals—plotters, printers, memory storage, and so forth—were interrelated. We wanted to be able to offer our customers the integral parts that could be combined into an entire system. At that time, industry efforts in printing were directed toward adapting the large multiuser system printers for use with minicomputers. But these mainframe system printers were notoriously unreliable and expensive both to purchase and to maintain.

Laser Technology

In the mid-1970s, working with Canon, HP began to develop laser printers that would work with our minicomputers. We wagered that customers soon would demand greater reliability, faster output, and better print quality. Laser technology would provide this. In 1982 HP introduced its first laser printer. We used licensed Canon electrophotographic technology but designed and built the product ourselves. The HP 2680 was about the size of a refrigerator and still expensive at about $100,000. But it was rugged and quiet. Using plain 8.5-by-11-inch paper, it was capable of very high resolution and high speed. It was a step in the right direction, and it created constructive ties between Canon and HP.

In the 1980s, with the emergence of the personal computer market, a new opportunity appeared. People with personal computers on their desks wanted easy and direct access to their printers. The Japanese quickly capitalized on this trend, producing two types of impact printers—inexpensive dot-matrix devices and slightly more expensive daisy-wheel printers. HP had no expertise in impact printers, but our work with Canon on minicomputer laser printers and our early development work on ink jet (well under way at this point) made us realize that the future of printing would be nonimpact. The field was wide open for product innovations.

LaserJet

Though it was traditional for HP to invent its own technology, Canon already had the printer engines we needed. With these engines, we saw we could build a relatively inexpensive laser printer for personal computers. We introduced the first LaserJet in March 1984. Nothing like it existed previously. It was small, fast, flexible, and reliable, and it delivered high-quality printing at an affordable price. The first LaserJet created a totally new printer market (similar to what handheld calculators had done twelve years before).

Right from the beginning, we recognized that the LaserJet printer, at $3,495, was going to be extremely popular. So we decided to distribute it using the small HP salesforce that focused on resellers. This avenue of distribution has been a major competitive advantage for HP during the past ten years.

"More for less" became the goal for each new LaserJet model. This objective reveals a lesson learned from our experience with calculators. For many years we continued to introduce increasingly sophisticated calculators with greater capabilities at greater cost to consumers. Meanwhile, our competitors were offering basic features at a lower price. For the mass market, basic features were sufficient, and the lower-priced models decreased HP's calculator market share. The sophisticated HP calculators sold to customers who needed more advanced capabilities—but we lost a large portion of the marketplace. With LaserJet printers, we decided that each revision would offer our customers greater capability at a lower price than its predecessor.

The LaserJet II was introduced in 1987. It outsold all other brands of laser printers worldwide (and there were many by this time). Improvements included better print quality and graphics capabilities. Best of all, it offered something that today seems almost ridiculously simple—correct-order paper output.

Two years later, HP introduced a product that was completely unexpected—the LaserJet IIP. The IIP was less sophisticated and substantially less expensive. It had all the print-quality, reliability, paper-handling, font, and graphics features of the II, but it was priced more than $1,000 less than its predecessor. We couldn't make them fast enough.

The long-expected LaserJet III was introduced in early 1990. It offered desktop-publishing-like typeface and graphics capabilities far beyond its predecessors.

Charles Tung, an engineer in the Boise lab, had developed and patented a way to more finely control the timing and duration of the firing of the printer's laser. This allowed variation in the size and placement of dots of toner on the printed page, creating a dramatic increase in print quality. The LaserJet III, at $2,395, cost less than the II and less than competing products. It took a year for the first clone that imitated Charles Tung's resolution-enhancement technology to enter the market.

Innovation continues apace. LaserJet now has become a universally recognized brand name for desktop laser printers, much like other brands such as Kleenex, Xerox, Band-aid, and Levi's evolved to characterize entire product categories.

The Ink-Jet Story

The story of HP's ink-jet printer business began in 1978 with a chance discovery at our corporate labs in Palo Alto. An engineer working on developing thin-film technology for integrated-circuit applications was testing the response of thin film to electrical stimulation. The electricity superheated the medium, and droplets of fluid lying under the film were expelled. An idea was born. What if we could finely control these jets of fluid? Large industrial ink-jet marking devices already existed, but up to this point only crude printing of quite large characters for industrial purposes was practical. Suddenly it looked like this marking technology could be miniaturized. And it had the advantages of requiring very little power to print and of being inherently inexpensive to manufacture.

As was the case with laser printers, the advent of the personal computer made the market opportunity clear. Only this time there were no other suppliers of ink-jet technology, and we knew we could make a significant contribution in this area.

Ink-jet technology offered HP the opportunity to

replace the least expensive printers in the market—serial dot-matrix impact printers—with products that were superior in every way. Ink jet had the potential for better print quality, quieter operation, extremely low power consumption, and eventually, high-quality, low-cost color.

ThinkJet

In 1980 the first HP thermal ink-jet product program began, and by 1982 we had designed the key element—a disposable printhead. In 1984 we introduced a thermal ink-jet printer called the ThinkJet—a small, rugged machine that printed on a special coated paper. With ninety-six dots per square inch, it was a completely new technology in a market dominated by noisy impact printers.

Much to our surprise, sales did not meet our expectations. We went to our customers to find out why, and they told us they wanted better print quality, a variety of typefaces, and the ability to print on any kind of paper. We went back to the drawing board.

Maverick

Our new ink-jet printer project was code-named "Maverick." It resulted in a product capable of 300 dots per square inch that offered a choice of fonts and had the capability of handling plain paper. But the product would have to sell for $1,500, which was too expensive for a personal printer. The project was canceled. This was a low point for our ink-jet R&D team. But, despite extreme disappointment, the team regrouped to try again.

DeskJet

Our customers had made it clear. They wanted an ink-jet product with near laser-print quality for under $1,000. The development group began with simple objectives: high quality, low price, and a twenty-two-month production schedule. This time, R&D, manufacturing, and marketing worked together right from the beginning in cross-functional teams. Decisions were made at the lowest possible level. Manufacturability was built into the product as it was being developed, and user focus groups helped keep us on track, concentrating on customer needs every step of the way.

There were difficult moments. We had printhead problems, dry-time problems, print-quality problems, but in six months we had a breadboard and a paper path mechanism with front loading and delivery, a combination of inventiveness and customer orientation. And our customers were satisfied with our improved print quality.

Our customer research showed that everyone preferred DeskJet's printing capabilities over dot matrix.

But $1,000 was a lot to spend on a personal printer when a dot matrix cost $350 to $500. We had no illusions about our need to lower the price. But because we carried all the development and manufacturing costs ourselves, we had to wait to bring the price down until the volume grew sufficiently.

The death knell of the dot-matrix printer tolled in 1990 when HP, supported by a rapidly decreasing cost structure, began a series of price cuts on its DeskJet printers that brought the entry-level list price from $995 for the original DeskJet to $365 in 1993. By 1994, that entry-level DeskJet (the DeskJet 540), superior to the original in every way, not only listed for $365, it offered a color-printing upgrade.

DeskJet single-handedly created the revolution in color printing. Prior to the introduction of the color DeskJet 500C in 1991, color printers were expensive, purchased only by users whose special needs justified the price. Our market research clearly showed that customers were not looking for color printers. Asked to prioritize their requirements for printers, customers consistently put color printing way down the list. But, when we asked, "If we satisfied all your black printing requirements and offered you the ability to print in color as well for little or no price penalty, would you buy such a printer?" the overwhelming response was "Yes." Our customers didn't want color printers, but they were very interested in printers that could print in color too. In short, HP should offer color as a feature.

In 1991, approximately 360,000 nonimpact "color" printers were sold worldwide by all vendors. In 1994 HP alone sold almost 4 million "color" printers. Today, all DeskJet printers can also print in color.

Quality

The essence of customer satisfaction at Hewlett-Packard is our commitment to *quality*, a commitment that begins in our laboratories and extends into every phase of our operations.

I think perhaps HP had more reason than other companies to emphasize quality. Early on we had decided to concentrate on developing and manufacturing electronic test and measuring instruments, and these instruments were used by our customers to test and measure the quality of their own products and processes. We therefore had a strong incentive to do a superior job.

Over the years we have spent a good deal of time looking at how we could improve quality. One method we found very effective was to lay out our production lines so that the area devoted to the final testing of a product was very close to the final assembly area. If the test crew detected any problem in the finished product, they could immediately and directly tell the assembly people without having to go through complicated procedures.

This was very much like what has come to be known

as a "quality circle" because here were people working closely together with effective, informal communication. We found over time that many good ideas emerged from this informal exchange among our test and assembly people, and this helped to keep an emphasis on quality and productivity.

Today, we are all familiar with the accomplishments of Japanese industry in producing quality products. In recent years Japan's automobiles, radios, television sets, recording equipment, and many other products have earned a worldwide reputation for quality and reliability. Our own experiences with the Japanese have contributed in important ways to the high quality of our Hewlett-Packard products.

Japanese Joint Venture

In 1963 we formed a joint venture with a company in Japan, a company that had been involved in process instrumentation and had some compatibility with our product line. When we were first considering the venture, which became known as Yokogawa-Hewlett-Packard or YHP, and now is Hewlett-Packard Japan, I visited Japan and spent a couple of weeks with the Yokogawa people. This was at a time when Japan's manufacturing and managerial skills were not up to our own, and when we started I concluded that if it were going to be successful, it needed to be managed our way rather than the Yokogawa way. The Japanese agreed, and so during YHP's formative years it was managed by one of our people, and it successfully adopted some of the things that had worked well for us in the United States.

At that time HP was structured into many relatively small divisions. Each year we got all the division managers together and spent two or three days reporting, comparing notes, evaluating performance, and so forth. One of our sessions always had to do with quality. We kept a record on the failure rate of every HP product and another record on our warranty costs.

During the first few years of our Japanese joint venture, the YHP general manager, an American, came to the meetings and reported along with all of our other managers. YHP's performance was usually just about in the middle. It was neither at the top nor at the bottom in product-failure rates or warranty costs.

After this had gone on for some years, a bright young Japanese manager, Kenzo Sasaoka, who was doing good work over there, cornered Bill Hewlett and me one day. He said, "Why don't you let me run YHP? You send an American manager to us to oversee our work. We spend a lot of time—in fact, waste a lot of time—talking to him, and if something goes wrong, he's the fellow we blame. We really think we can do better." So we said, "Okay, you go ahead—you run the operation and we'll see how it goes."

The following year, YHP grew at a faster rate than ever before, and it showed improvement in the quality of its product. It started to move up toward the top of the HP list, and soon after, the manager returned with some amazing data on YHP quality. The failure rates on the products it was building were better than those of any of our other divisions. And a few years following that, in 1982, it received Japan's coveted Deming Prize for productivity and quality. This prize, the object of intense competition among Japanese firms, is named for Dr. W. Edwards Deming, an American statistician who helped the Japanese improve their product quality in the years following World War II.

Here is an example of what YHP was able to do. We had been making printed circuit boards in various parts of the company. Our best failure rates were about four in a thousand. We thought that was fairly good—a little less than 0.5 percent. And that was the rate we found a lot of other companies were achieving. Our Japanese unit, on the other hand, came in with a failure rate on its printed circuit boards of only *ten per million.* That's four hundred times better than anything we had been able to do.

Obviously that shook up a lot of people—and changed a lot of thinking—within the company. It clearly showed that our targets on quality just were nowhere near what could be achieved. The positive result was that the thinking and the work they were doing at YHP were soon reflected all over the company. We were able to raise quality targets in many divisions and locations, far beyond anything we thought could have been done before. I had often seen the people in our operation at YHP spend considerable time making sure that every adjustment was done just as accurately as possible. The same adjustments were done at HP in Palo Alto just as quickly as possible to get them just barely within the limits specified. This came about because people in Palo Alto were on profit sharing and people in Japan were not. I pointed this out to Kenzo Sasaoka, our manager in Japan, and he said that I had shown him the way—that gains in quality come from meticulous attention to detail and every step in the manufacturing process must be done as *carefully* as possible, not as *quickly* as possible. This sounds simple, but it is achieved only if everyone in the organization is dedicated to quality.

Chapter 9

Trust in People

IF AN ORGANIZATION IS to maximize its efficiency and success, a number of requirements must be met. One is that the most capable people available should be selected for each assignment within the organization. Especially in a technical business where the rate of progress is rapid, a continuing program of education must be undertaken and maintained. Techniques that are relevant today will be outdated in the future, and every person in the organization must be continually looking for new and better ways to do his or her work.

Another requirement is that a high degree of enthusiasm should be encouraged at all levels; in particular, the people in high management positions must not only be enthusiastic themselves, they must be able to engender enthusiasm among their associates. There can be no place for halfhearted interest or halfhearted effort.

From the beginning, Bill Hewlett and I have had a strong belief in people. We believe that people *want* to do a good job and that it is important for them to enjoy their work at Hewlett-Packard. We try to make it possible for our people to feel a real sense of accomplishment in their work.

Closely coupled with this is our strong belief that individuals be treated with consideration and respect and that their achievements be recognized. It has always been important to Bill and me to create an environment in which people have a chance to be their best, to realize their potential, and to be recognized for their achievements.

Each person in our company is important, and every job is important. In the highly technical fields in which we operate, little details often make the difference between a quality product and one that isn't as good. So what we've tried to engender among all our people is the attitude that it is each individual's business to do the best job he or she can. I recall the time, many years ago, when I was walking around a machine shop, accompanied by the shop's manager. We stopped briefly to watch a machinist making a polished plastic mold die. He had spent a long time polishing it and was taking a final cut at it. Without thinking, I reached down and wiped it with my finger. The machinist said, "Get your finger off my die!" The manager quickly asked him, "Do you know who this is?" To which the machinist replied, "I don't care!" He was right and I told him so. He had an important job and was proud of his work.

The way an organization is structured affects individual motivation and performance. There are military-type organizations in which the person at the top issues an order and it is passed on down the line until the person at the bottom does as he or she is told without question or reason. This is precisely the type of organization we at HP did not want . . . and do not want. We feel our objectives can best be achieved by people who understand and support them and who are allowed flexibility in working toward common goals in ways that they help determine are best for their operation and their organization.

The close relationships among HP people encouraged a form of participatory management that supported individual freedom and initiative while emphasizing commonness of purpose and teamwork. In the early years we were all working on the same problems. We solicited and used ideas from wherever we could get them. The net result was that each employee felt that he or she was a member of the team.

As the company grew, we could no longer take teamwork for granted. We had to try to emphasize and strengthen it. That's one of the reasons we didn't single out divisions or groups that were doing particularly well. And why benefits such as profit sharing are provided not to selected individuals or groups but to all eligible employees. It's imperative that there be a strong spirit of helpfulness and cooperation among all elements of the company and that this spirit be recognized and respected as a cornerstone of the HP Way.

When we were small and insignificant and had to hire the best people we could find, we had to train them and then hope they would work out. We wanted our people to share our goals of making a profit and a contribution. We in turn felt a responsibility to provide them with opportunity and job security to the best of our ability. Thus, we made an early and important decision: We did not want to be a "hire and fire"—a company that would seek large, short-term contracts, employ a great many people for the duration of the contract, and at its completion let those people go. This type of operation is often the quickest and most efficient way to get a big job accomplished. But Bill and I didn't want to operate that way. We wanted to be in business for the long haul, to have a company built around a stable and dedicated workforce.

We were very close to our employees. We understood their jobs and shared much of their lives with them. We also were learning which of our people had management potential, although sometimes we learned the hard way. Once we promoted a man, a good worker, to be the manager of our machine shop. A few days later he came to see me. He said he was having a tough time managing and wanted me to come out to the shop and tell his people that he was their boss. "If I have to do that," I said, "you don't deserve to be their boss."

Another early experience, again related to our close association with our people, was the case of an employee who contracted tuberculosis and was required to take a leave of absence for two years. This had a serious effect on his family, and although we were able to provide some financial help, we determined that this type of problem should never be repeated. Consequently, we established a program of catastrophic medical insurance to protect our employees and their families. In the late 1940s this type of coverage was virtually unknown.

The interest Bill and I and our families had in the welfare of HP employees was reflected in some early practices and customs. Immediately after World War II our employment dropped, but by 1950 it had grown back up to about two hundred. At that time my wife, Lucile, started the practice of buying a wedding gift for every employee who married and a baby blanket for every family having a baby. This continued for ten years or so, until the practice fell victim to the company's rapid growth and decentralization.

In fact, Lucile instigated many traditions that served to enhance the family atmosphere at HP and helped create a sense of belonging in our young enterprise. Both she and Flora Hewlett were constantly working on behalf of the company. As I said earlier, Lucile served as our secretary and bookkeeper for the first several years of our operation. She contributed not only time and energy but also a viewpoint and a sense of caring that, eventually, became a vital component of the spirit that defines everything we do.

Growth also affected the size and nature of company picnics. Bill and I considered picnics an important part of the HP Way, and in the early days we had an annual picnic in the Palo Alto area for all our people and their families. It was a big event, one largely planned and carried out by our employees themselves. The menu consisted of New York steaks, hamburgers, Mexican beans or frijoles, green salad, garlic French bread, and beer. The company bought the food and beer. It became customary for the machine shop people to barbeque the steaks and burgers, with other departments responsible for other parts of the menu. Bill and I and other senior executives served the food, giving us the opportunity to meet all of the employees and their families.

In the early 1950s the company bought a parcel of land, called Little Basin, in the redwood country about an hour's drive from Palo Alto. We converted part of it into a recreation area, large enough to have a picnic with two thousand people or more. We also made it available year around for our employees and their families to go overnight camping. This was such a popular benefit that we decided, later on, to duplicate the idea in other parts of the world where we had concentrations

At a company picnic in the 1960s, Dave Packard, center, serves steaks.

of HP people. In Colorado we bought some land in the Rockies next to Estes Park, and in Massachusetts on the seashore. In Scotland we bought a small lake, featuring good fishing (and possible sightings of the Loch Ness monster), and in southern Germany we bought land suitable for skiing.

As the company grew, each division would have its own picnic. Bill and I and some of the other HP executives would try to attend as many of these as we could, since they gave us the opportunity to meet and chat with many employees, both in the United States and in Europe. By the late 1960s the company had grown so large, and there were so many picnics, that it was difficult to continue this tradition, and today, of course, it would be impossible. But annual picnics continue to occur at HP sites throughout the world.

Sharing

The underlying principle of HP's personnel policies became the concept of sharing—sharing the responsibilities for defining and meeting goals, sharing in company ownership through stock purchase plans, sharing in profits, sharing the opportunities for personal and professional development, and even sharing the burdens created by occasional downturns in business.

Our employee benefit programs reflect this concept of sharing. The programs take various forms around the world, each country organization having its own set of benefits tailored to its own laws and traditions.

In the United States and many other countries, employees participate in stock purchase plans and in cash profit sharing. U.S. employees with more than six months of service are eligible for profit sharing, and each year receive amounts calculated on the company's pretax earnings. Over the years this payout has been as high as 9.9 percent and as low as 4.1 percent of base salary. Since the company has always been profitable, the program has continued uninterrupted since we started it in the 1950s.

Another example of sharing, though in a much different way, occurred in 1970. Because of a downturn in the U.S. economy, our incoming orders were running at a rate quite a bit less than our production capability. We were faced with the prospect of a 10 percent layoff. Rather than a layoff, however, we tried a different tack. We went to a schedule of working nine days out of every two weeks—a 10 percent cut in work schedule with a corresponding 10 percent cut in pay. This applied to virtually all our U.S. factories, as well as to all executives and corporate staff. At the end of a six-month period, the order rate was up again and everyone returned to a full work schedule. Some said they enjoyed the long weekends even though they had to tighten their belts a little. The net result of this program was that effectively all shared the burden of the recession, good people were not released into a very tough job market, and we had our highly qualified workforce in place when business improved.

I should point out that this program was in response to a temporary situation, one likely to last for no more than a year or two. It was a short-term solution to a short-term problem and did not represent a commitment to providing absolute tenure status for our people.

Since 1970, of course, there have been other economic recessions in the United States and in most other countries. Generally speaking, we've been able to ride out these recessions by transferring production from some areas to others and by instituting temporary work-reduction programs at a few locations. As we moved into the early 1990s, however, it became clear that HP, like almost every other American manufacturer, would need to reduce staff. "Downsizing" is today's popular euphemism, but in any event, our need to cut was considerably less than that of most manufacturers, especially those in the computer industry. We had already taken steps at HP to reduce corporate bureaucracy and to emphasize decentralization. We accomplished most staff reductions through early-retirement programs and a program of voluntary severance, offering a generous financial package to people willing to leave the company.

The rapid changes in technology make educational and training activities a necessity for our people. Many of our corporate-sponsored educational programs are on specific technical subjects, while others emphasize more general skills. As a corporation, we spend about

$200 million each year in developing and providing courses for our employees. And the cost of allowing people time off from work and supporting them in outside, job-related courses adds another $300 million or so. Part of that expense is supporting college work, often aimed at an advanced degree.

To some, education means unnecessary sacrifice; to others it means the prospect of opportunity for increased contribution and greater personal satisfaction. Fortunately, the latter view has prevailed at Hewlett-Packard. The vast majority of our people have recognized the value of education and self-development, not only in enhancing their careers but also in making meaningful contributions to the company's progress.

So going all the way back to the beginning of the company, Bill and I have placed great faith and trust in HP people. We expect them to be open and honest in their dealings with others, and we trust they will readily accept responsibility.

I learned, early in my career, of some of the problems that can be caused by a company's lack of trust in its people. In the late 1930s, when I was working for General Electric in Schenectady, the company was making a big thing of plant security. I'm sure others were, too. GE was especially zealous about guarding its tool and parts bins to make sure employees didn't steal anything. Faced with this obvious display of distrust, many employees set out to prove it justified, walking off with tools or parts whenever they could. Eventually, GE tools and parts were scattered all around town, including the attic of the house in which a number of us were living. In fact, we had so much equipment up there that when we threw the switch, the lights on the entire street would dim.

The irony in all of this is that many of the tools and parts were being used by their GE "owners" to work on either job-related projects or skill-enhancing hobbies—activities that would likely improve their performance on the job.

When HP got under way, the GE memories were still strong and I determined that our parts bins and storerooms should always be open. Sometimes not everyone gets the word, however, which accounts for an incident that occurred some years later. Coming into the plant one weekend to do some work, Bill Hewlett stopped off at a company storeroom to pick up a microscope. Finding the equipment cage locked, he broke open the latch and left a note insisting that the room not be locked again.

Keeping storerooms and parts bins open was advantageous to HP in two important ways. From a practical standpoint, the easy access to parts and tools helped product designers and others who wanted to work out new ideas at home or on weekends. A second reason, less tangible but important, is that the open bins and storerooms were a symbol of trust, a trust that is central to the way HP does business.

Our policy of open storerooms continues. Although

production stock is restricted, lab stock (a relatively small supply of our best parts and equipment) is still generally open.

Flexible Hours

Perhaps the most widely publicized example of trust at HP is the company's program of flexible work hours. It was initiated at our plant in Böblingen, Germany, in 1967, and we were the first company in the United States to use it. It is now in wide use throughout HP and throughout industry. Under the HP program, an individual may come to work very early in the morning or perhaps as late as 9:00 A.M., then leave after working a standard number of hours. It is not appropriate for all jobs, but certainly for most.

To my mind, flextime is the essence of respect for and trust in people. It says that we both appreciate that our people have busy personal lives and that we trust them to devise, with their supervisor and work group, a schedule that is personally convenient yet fair to others.

Tolerance for the differing needs of individuals is another element of the HP Way. On occasion, situations arise in which people have personal problems that temporarily affect their performance and attitude, and it is important that people in these circumstances be treated with sensitivity and understanding while the problems are being resolved.

Many companies have a policy stating that once employees leave the company, they are not eligible for reemployment. Over the years we have had a number of people leave because opportunities seemed greater elsewhere. We've always taken the view that as long as they have not worked for a direct competitor, and if they have a good work record, they are welcomed back. They know the company, need no retraining, and usually are happier and better motivated for having had the additional experience. Several years ago one of our senior executives left HP for what he considered a greater opportunity. He later returned, and although he had been gone for some years, he quickly resumed his career with us and earned increasing management responsibility until his retirement.

Some people have left HP and have successfully started their own companies. There are at least a dozen of these entrepreneurs and their companies now employ more than forty thousand people. Are we upset that they left us? On the contrary, Bill and I understand and respect their entrepreneurial spirit, and we are pleased and proud that they once worked with us and have done so well. We're also flattered that in building their companies, they have adopted many of the management principles and practices embodied in the HP Way.

Chapter 10

Growing the Organization

AN ORGANIZATIONAL STRUCTURE, once created, should be flexible and responsive to the developing needs of the organization and changes in the marketplace.

In the case of Hewlett-Packard, we did not much concern ourselves with organizational matters until well into the 1950s. There was no need to. We had a well-defined line of related products, designed and manufactured in one location, sold through an established network of sales representatives, and had a highly centralized company in which management was organized on a fundamental basis with vice presidents for marketing, manufacturing, R&D, and finance. As the company continued its steady growth and began to diversify, Bill and I realized we would have to consider some sort of decentralized strategy in order to retain our emphasis on individual responsibility and achievement.

We also worried that the personal elements of the HP Way might disappear.

Divisionalization first occurred in our product development laboratory where, as I have mentioned, we divided our development activities into four groups, each with responsibility for its own family of products and each headed by a manager reporting to Barney Oliver, vice president of research and development. That was in 1957. Other divisionalizing steps soon followed, spurred by our geographic expansion that established manufacturing operations in Colorado and Germany, and by our early acquisitions of new businesses.

By the mid-1960s we had more than a dozen operating divisions, each an integrated, self-sustaining orga-

Left to right: Bill Hewlett, Barney Oliver, and Lee De Forest, the inventor of the vacuum tube, at HP Labs in 1957.

nization responsible for developing, manufacturing, and marketing its own products. A primary goal in setting up these divisions was to give each one considerable autonomy, creating an environment that fostered individual motivation, initiative, and creativity, and that gave a wide latitude of freedom in working toward common goals and objectives. We wanted to avoid bureaucracy and to be sure that problem-solving decisions be made as close as possible to the level where the problem occurred. We also wanted each division to retain and nurture the kind of intimacy, the caring for people, and the ease of communication that were characteristic of the company when it was smaller.

Over the years Bill Hewlett and I had speculated many times about the optimum size of a company. We did not believe that growth was important for its own sake. However, continuous growth was essential for us to achieve our other objectives and to remain competitive. Since we participate in fields of advanced and rapidly changing technologies, to remain static is to lose ground. Also, we depended on attracting high-caliber people to the company, people wanting to align their careers only with a company that offered ample opportunity for personal growth and progress.

By the late 1950s, the need for diversification was clear. We were becoming the largest supplier in most of the major segments of the electronic-instrumentation business. But these segments, in total, were growing at only 6 percent per year, whereas we had been growing, out of our profits, at 22 percent. Obviously, that kind of growth could not continue without diversification. In 1961 we formed an affiliate, HP Associates, to engage in solid-state research and development. And later, in 1966, we created the HP Laboratories, a corporate lab engaged in advanced research activities to help lead the company into new technologies and product diversification.

Growth by Acquisition

Bill and I had no desire to see HP become a conglomerate, since, as I've already pointed out, more companies die from indigestion than starvation. In the 1960s, however, some opportunities came along for us to acquire companies whose technologies and products complemented our own. Our first acquisition, the F. L. Moseley Company, had occurred in 1958. Located in Pasadena, California, Moseley made X-Y recorders and other instruments that were a good complement to our own product line. The company had been founded by Francis Moseley, a very inventive engineer who later served as a valued member of our board of directors. His management philosophy and practices were very similar to our own.

The largest firm we acquired in the 1960s was the Sanborn Company, in Waltham, Massachusetts. Sanborn, which had 950 employees and annual sales of more than $16 million, produced electrocardiographs and other test and measurement instruments used by the medical profession. The acquisition, accomplished through an exchange of stock, gave us an entry into the medical field, which grew into a major market for HP. We later acquired a smaller company, F&M Scientific, which provided us with a similar entry into the field of instrumentation for chemical analysis.

While acquisitions are often useful in expanding a company's technologies and gaining a quick entry into new markets, they are not without their problems. Chief among these is the difficulty in blending two cultures, operating philosophies, and management styles. It is difficult—understandably so—for the management of the acquired company to give up its independence. And the acquiring company usually finds that the task of providing guidance and resources to its new addition requires much more management time and energy than it ever anticipated.

I remember the problems one particular acquisition caused us back in the mid-1960s. We acquired a company called Autodynamics, headquartered in Sacramento, California. It specialized in using ultrasonic energy to detect flaws in metals. This was before the use of ultrasound in medical applications. It had a product called Mustang, a full rack of electronic equipment. In the center of the rack the company had screwed a metal mustang taken from a Ford Mustang, which was new at the time. I remember looking at the flashy chrome horse mounted on the electronic equipment and thinking that it didn't quite fit HP's way of thinking about our products as scientific instruments.

There were other problems as well. The company had a contract to build some ultrasound machines for testing rocket casings. We inherited the contract and soon learned that the machine wouldn't do what the company said it would do. We rescued that contract with money and some technical expertise from HP Labs. But within eight months or so, we folded up the whole operation.

Changes in Sales Organization

In the 1960s we made still other organizational changes, these related to our field sales activity in the United States. Since the early days of the company, sales of HP products had been handled through a network of sales representative firms located in various parts of the country. These firms, about ten in number, represented and sold the products of other, noncompeting electronics manufacturers as well as those of HP.

Though this arrangement had worked very well, some problems had begun to arise in the early 1960s, most of them stemming from HP's rapid growth. Sales of our products represented an increasing share, in some cases a disproportionate share, of the sales representatives' business. There was also the potential, with the growing diversification of product lines, of competitive conflicts arising among products sold by a single representative. It was, in short, time to establish our own sales organization. We accomplished this not by breaking ties with our existing representatives and building an organization from scratch but by approaching most of our representatives to see if they would be interested in becoming sales divisions of Hewlett-Packard. The response was positive, and virtually all of these firms agreed to be acquired by HP, either by an exchange of stock or by cash purchase. Noel Eldred, our vice president of marketing, had worked with the representatives for several years and played a key role in our negotiations with them.

I have mentioned that by the mid-1960s we had more than a dozen operating divisions, each responsible for developing, manufacturing, and marketing their own products. In addition, the acquisition of our U.S. sales representatives added another group of units reporting into Palo Alto. We had expanded our international markets as well. In Europe, we had set up our own sales organization headquartered in Geneva and had established manufacturing plants in Germany and England. And in Japan, our joint-venture company had become operational. So within a few short years we had grown from a highly centralized, rather narrowly focused company into one with many widely dispersed divisions and activities. And our family of products had substantially increased, both in size and diversity.

This transition presented us with a good many management challenges. Among these was the problem of staffing some of our new operating units with effective managers. We were successful in doing this, thanks in large part to recruiting efforts and training programs.

We had well-qualified people within HP to fill key management positions.

As the company became more decentralized, our objectives and policies did not change in any significant way. At that time we were still largely in the business of general-purpose electronic instrumentation, and our growth was derived almost entirely from new products. We continued to focus our efforts on those technical areas where we thought we could make a good contribution, and we were not taking on any new projects just for the sake of growing.

As time went on, some of our older divisions grew to a substantial size, producing many different products and employing as many as 1,500 people. At that point, lines of communication are stretched to the limit, management becomes more difficult, and people begin to lose their identification with the products and their pride in what the division is doing. So it became our policy, still observed today, to split off part of the division, giving it responsibility for an established, profitable product line and usually moving it to a new but nearby location. This "local decentralization," as I suppose it could be called, has been successfully implemented in California, Colorado, Massachusetts—virtually everywhere we have major facilities and operations.

In rapidly growing companies, organizational changes occur quite frequently, and in HP's case our next transition occurred in 1968. With the number of operating divisions and their product lines steadily increasing, we gradually adopted a group structure.

This involved combining, organizationally, divisions with related product lines and markets into a group headed by a group manager with a small staff. Each group was responsible for the coordination of divisional activities and the overall operations and financial performance of its members. We had two objectives: to enable compatible units to work together more effectively on a day-to-day basis, and to begin to decentralize some top-management functions so that the new groups would be responsible for some of the planning activities and other functions previously assigned to corporate vice presidents.

The group structure also extended to our field sales organization, where it had become difficult, if not impossible, for an HP sales engineer to understand and sell the entire line of HP products. Under the new structure, the sales engineer became the representative of a specific group, selling and supporting only that group's products.

As the company moved to a group structure, I stressed to our people that this change did not represent any deviation from our traditional philosophy of management. From the beginning we had a strong belief that groups of people should be given responsibility for specific areas of activity with wide latitude to develop their own plans and make their own decisions. Our new organization did not alter this basic concept, but strengthened it. By the early 1990s, HP had sixty-five divisions, organized into thirteen product groups.

The Perils of Centralization

It has been my experience that most business executives are quick to praise the concept of decentralization. But when it comes to their own organization, many are reluctant to adopt it. Perhaps the idea of turning over a portion of their authority to others is too unsettling. From personal experience I've learned that even widely decentralized companies should be alert to signs of cumbersome centralization.

HP had a real test in this regard. Beginning back in the 1970s, when it was clear that a good deal of our future business lay in computers and computer-related products, many HP managers began to look at IBM as the model company. IBM's organizational structure was highly centralized, and many thought that was the way to go. Another factor pushing the trend toward centralization was the new demands placed on the HP organization by the computer business. Prior to entering the computer field, the HP organization was structured for the instrument business, with decentralized divisions responsible for well-defined product lines and operating with a good amount of independence. This structure had worked very well for instruments, and some thought it could be applied with equal effectiveness to computers.

But working against that idea were two principal characteristics of the computer business. One, new to

HP, was the whole area of software. How do you organize to produce software? Where does it report? What types of people and skills do you need? Second, the computer business is a systems business. It requires many elements—software, mainframes, peripherals, operating systems—to be combined into saleable products supported by strong service and maintenance. Good coordination is essential.

HP responded to these challenges by trying various forms of organization. There were divisions, group structures, then various task forces, councils, and committees intended to improve coordination. Over time these efforts began to create a complicated bureaucracy. Problems needing prompt and intelligent decisions were being referred through level after level of management with unwieldy committees. Decisions were often postponed for weeks or even months.

By 1990, we faced a crisis. Committees had taken over the decision-making process at HP, and decision cycle times had ballooned. For example, one central committee, the Computer Business Executive Committee, was intended to achieve a better focus and coordination for computer activities. Instead, it was slowing vital decisions just as our company entered the lightning-fast competitive world of computers in the 1990s. In fact, the paralysis was spreading to areas of the company that had nothing to do with computers. That we were struggling was no secret; our stock had fallen to $25.

At that time Bill Hewlett and I, though we continued to be active on the board, no longer participated in the day-to-day management of the company. But we could not help but be aware of the problems. Thanks to the company's long-standing open door policy, we were receiving visits from troubled HP managers as well as an increasing number of letters from concerned employees. After a while, Bill and I actually began systematically to visit several HP facilities and meet with employees at all levels of the organization to find out what, really, was going on.

Eventually, we knew what we needed to do. Too many layers of management had been built into the organization. We reduced them. We brought a gifted younger manager, Lew Platt, into the executive committee as chief executive. His predecessor, John Young—the skilled executive who had managed the company's explosive growth through the late 1970s and 1980s—was part of the group that selected Lew. (In 1993, Lew was promoted once again to chairman of the board of Hewlett-Packard.)

Needless to say, the Computer Business Executive Committee was disbanded, as was much of the bureaucracy. Most important, computer operating units were given greater freedom to create their own plans and make their own decisions, resulting in a much more flexible and agile company.

By 1993, our stock was up to $70. As of this writing, it's over $100 and about to be split.

HP systems increasingly include products from different groups and divisions, and even though an organization is highly decentralized, its people should be regularly reminded that cooperation between individuals and coordinated efforts among operating units are essential to growth and success. Although we minimize corporate direction at HP, we consider ourselves one single company, with the flexibility of a small company and the strengths of a large one—the ability to draw on corporate resources and services; shared standards, values, and culture; common goals and objectives; and a single worldwide identity.

Chapter 11

Managing the Organization

NO OPERATING POLICY has contributed more to Hewlett-Packard's success than the policy of "management by objective." Although the term is relatively new to the lexicon of business, management by objective has been a fundamental part of HP's operating philosophy since the very early days of the company.

MBO, as it is frequently called, is the antithesis of management by control. The latter refers to a tightly controlled system of management of the military type, where people are assigned—and expected to do—specific jobs, precisely as they are told and without the need to know much about the overall objectives of the organization. Management by objective, on the other hand, refers to a system in which overall objectives are clearly stated and agreed upon, and which gives people the flexibility to work toward those goals in ways they determine best for their own areas of responsibility. It is the philosophy of decentralization in management and the very essence of free enterprise.

More and more companies are recognizing the very real benefits provided by decentralization and management by objective. They are also finding that the concept of people working together under common objectives and in an atmosphere of individual freedom is nothing new. It was demonstrated by Athens against Sparta more than twenty centuries ago. There is much evidence, both from history and from current business experience, to show that an organization offering opportunity for individual initiative performs better than organizations operating with corporate directives and tight controls.

I should point out that the successful practice of management by objective is a two-way street. Managers at all levels must be sure that their people clearly understand the overall objectives and goals of the company, as well as the specific goals of their particular division or department. Thus, managers have a strong obligation to foster good communication and mutual understanding. Conversely, their people must take sufficient interest in their work to want to plan it, to propose new solutions to old problems, and to jump in when they have something to contribute.

Peter Drucker, the well-known management consultant, expressed his thoughts on this subject in an interview in the spring 1993 issue of the *Harvard Business Review*. Drucker talks about what he calls the "Post-Capitalist Society." In this new society and corporate environment, Drucker says managers "will have to learn to manage in situations where you don't have command authority, where you are neither controlled nor controlling." He later points out that "in the traditional organization—the organization of the last 100 years—the skeleton, or internal structure, was a combination of rank and power. In the emerging organization, it has to be mutual understanding and responsibility."

Though Hewlett-Packard is hardly an emerging organization, mutual understanding and responsibility have been, for many years, key characteristics of the HP style of management.

Managers must be sure that their people clearly understand the objectives and specific goals of their division or department, as I have said. It is also essential that the manager have a thorough knowledge and understanding of the work of his or her group. This brings up the debate that has been carried on by businesspeople for many years. Some say good managers can manage anything; they can manage well without really knowing what they are trying to manage. It's the management skills that count.

I don't argue that the job can't be done that way, but I do argue strongly that the *best* job can be done when the manager has a genuine and thorough understanding of the work. I don't see how managers can even understand what standards to observe, what performance to require, and how to measure results unless they understand in some detail the specific nature of the work they are trying to supervise. We have held closely to this philosophy at HP and I hope will continue to do so.

We have a technique at HP for helping managers and supervisors know their people and understand the work their people are doing, while at the same time making themselves more visible and accessible to their people. It's called MBWA—"management by walking around." The term, a good one, was coined many years ago by one of our managers, though the technique itself goes back to my days at General Electric.

Solving the Ignitron Problem

As I mentioned earlier, when I was with GE in its vacuum-tube engineering department, it was having problems manufacturing ignitrons, and I was given the job of finding out why so many were failing during testing.

I learned everything I could about the causes of failure and decided to spend most of my time on the factory floor, making sure every step in the manufacturing process was done correctly. I found several instances where the written instructions provided the manufacturing people were inadequate, and I worked with them on each step in the process to make sure there were no mistakes. This painstaking attention to detail paid off, and every tube in the next batch passed its final test.

As I look back, my decision to work on that ignitron problem with the people in the factory had a profound influence on the management policies we developed for the Hewlett-Packard Company. That was the genesis of what has been called MBWA. I learned that quality requires minute attention to every detail, that everyone in an organization wants to do a good job, that written instructions are seldom adequate, and that personal involvement is essential.

We have found this personal involvement to be very important at all levels in the company. I also found it useful when I served in Washington as U.S. deputy secretary of defense.

At HP we discovered that the practices of MBWA and MBO were generally as effective at our overseas sites as they were in the United States. Our international divisions typically were started by seasoned HP managers who had grown up in the company and were well versed in our principles and practices.

Division reviews outside the United States usually occurred annually. Bill and I attended these meetings together. Our visits always included a walk around the facilities, giving us the opportunity to meet and chat informally with our employees and see the work they were doing.

The Open Door Policy

Straightforward as it sounds, there are some subtleties and requirements that go with MBWA. For one thing, not every manager finds it easy and natural to do. And if it's done reluctantly or infrequently, it just won't work. It needs to be frequent, friendly, unfocused, and unscheduled—but far from pointless. And since its principal aim is to seek out people's thoughts and opinions, it requires good *listening.*

Linked with MBWA is another important management practice at Hewlett-Packard, and a basic tenet of the HP Way. It's called the "open door policy." Like MBWA, this policy is aimed at building mutual trust and understanding, and creating an environment in which people feel free to express their ideas, opinions, problems, and concerns.

The open door encourages employees, should they have problems of either a personal or job-related nature, to discuss these with an appropriate manager. In the vast majority of cases, this will be the employee's immediate supervisor. But, should the employee be uncomfortable talking with the supervisor, he or she can go up the line to discuss misunderstandings or any other problems with a higher-level manager. We've found that people do not seem to be particularly averse to bringing up any problems or concerns they may have, and managers usually are able to find satisfactory solutions fairly quickly. It must be clearly understood by supervisors and managers that people using the open door are not to be subjected to reprisals or to any other adverse consequences.

I am occasionally asked the extent to which the open door policy is used at HP. It is used quite frequently, and in response to another question, both Bill Hewlett and I have each participated in open door communications with employees, usually about issues of general concern rather than personal grievances.

The open door policy is very important at HP because it characterizes the management style to which we are dedicated. It means managers are available, open, and receptive. Everyone at HP, including the CEO, works in open-plan, doorless offices. This ready availability has its drawbacks in that interruptions are always possible. But at HP we've found that the benefits of accessibility far outweigh the disadvantages. The open door policy is an integral part of the management-by-objective philosophy. Also, it is a procedure that encourages and, in fact, ensures that the communication flow be upward as well as downward.

HP is considered unusual in that during the first eighteen years of our existence, we operated without a personnel department. This is not because Bill and I had any negative feelings toward personnel departments or personnel managers but because of the emphasis we placed on relationships between our managers and their people, particularly the need for managers to be accessible to their people and to be sensitive to their problems and concerns. We felt that the presence of a personnel function might supplant, or interfere with, this direct manager-employee relationship. So in 1957, when we established a corporate personnel department, we were careful in defining its role and responsibilities. It was to support management, not supplant it.

Visitors to HP often notice and comment to us about

another facet of the HP Way—our informality and our use of first names in addressing each other. Bill and I have always believed that we all operate more effectively and comfortably in a truly informal and first-name atmosphere. Like all large companies, HP has organization charts. And, as in growing companies everywhere, our charts undergo frequent changes. We think of them only as providing a general guideline to the structure of an HP organization, whether it be a division, a group, or the corporation itself. In no way do charts dictate the channels of communication used by HP people. We want our people to communicate with one another in a simple and direct way, guided by common sense rather than by lines and boxes on a chart. To get the job done, an individual is expected to seek information from the most likely source.

It's important that individuals have their performance evaluated on a regular basis. It's also important that they be kept up to date on how their particular division or department is performing. To fill this broader need, HP managers make good use of coffee talks and other informal employee gatherings. Employee publications, films, and videotapes are useful communications media, but nothing beats personal, two-way communication for fostering cooperation and teamwork and for building an attitude of trust and understanding among employees.

Management Succession

An important responsibility of managers is the selection and training of their potential successors. Management succession is especially critical at the upper levels of an organization, where a manager may be responsible for a wide scope of complex activities involving the expenditure of many millions of dollars and the efforts of many thousands of people.

During the early years of Hewlett-Packard, as with any small company, we didn't give much thought to management succession. But as the company grew, the selection of the best-qualified person to fill a specific position became much more challenging. The growing size and diversity of HP's operations led to a similar growth in management positions and made it important that we develop an effective management selection process.

The process has several elements, but its roots are in our long-established policy of management by objective. Under the MBO principle, managers at all levels are given an opportunity to show their abilities—to develop plans, to make and evaluate decisions, and to provide leadership for their people. Managers often have many responsibilities, and perhaps this is no better illustrated than in the job of managing an HP division or business unit. These managers, under MBO and our decentralized structure, are given full product-line responsibility and P&L accountability. In effect they are running a small business—with all that that entails. And most are doing it reasonably early in their careers. This tends to produce generation after generation of young managers already experienced in running an HP business.

We have always tried to have our top-management team become acquainted with the younger managers in the company. One of the ways we did this in the past was through our divisional review meetings. Each division would be visited at least once a year by Bill and me, plus Barney Oliver, Noel Eldred, and other top managers. We spent a full day reviewing the division's operations, concentrating on its product-development programs. At these meetings we asked both the division manager and the key people reporting to him to make a presentation. This gave us an opportunity to appraise the abilities of the younger managers and also to assess how well their bosses were carrying out their training and development responsibilities. A dinner in conjunction with the meeting also helped us become acquainted in a more informal way with many of the division managers.

Today it is not possible for HP's top management to conduct an annual review of each of the company's many divisions. Instead the divisions are regularly reviewed by their respective group management, and the group's operations by top management. Though the format is different, the inherent benefits derived from the review process have been preserved. Starting many years ago, Bill and I established a similar review process within the company's board of directors meetings. It is the usual practice at each board meeting to have an organizational unit within HP, such as a product group, a sales unit, or a corporate department, give a presentation about its area of operation. This has the advantage of enabling our outside directors to become more familiar both with the company and with many of the people who manage it. Eventually, some of the more senior HP managers themselves are elected to the board, and it is important that each director become acquainted with these managers and their abilities prior to the election.

In recent years the company has developed additional, more structured ways of evaluating middle managers and their potential for greater responsibility. On a regular basis the CEO, now Lew Platt, gathers his top managers for a lengthy review of group management performance. They discuss each group's profit generation, asset utilization, revenue growth, product quality, customer satisfaction, personnel issues, and other matters for which the group manager is responsible. Lew also meets periodically with a committee of the board of directors, the Organization Review and Nominating Committee, to review the performance of key managers.

Promoting from Within

I have always felt that the most successful companies have a practice of promoting from within. Until the 1960s, when we entered the computer business, it was rare to find a key manager who had not grown up within the company. Our entry into the computer business changed that a bit. We needed to acquire some expertise in computer science, and a good part of that expertise was available only from outside the company. Most of those who joined us, in addition to making important contributions to our strength in computer technology, adapted quite readily to the HP culture. A few did not and chose to leave.

Long before we reached retirement, Bill and I had been thinking and talking about who might succeed us. John Young was our choice for many reasons, and in 1977 the president's title passed to him. Bill remained as CEO, and I as chairman. This provided a good transition to the time when Bill retired in 1978 and John became CEO in addition to being president. He served in this dual capacity until 1992, when he turned sixty and retired from the company. John had done an outstanding job for us. John's retirement allowed the board to elect Lew Platt to succeed him while Bill and I were still around to manage the transition. Lew now serves as chairman, CEO, and president.

Virtually all the managers who have served, or are

serving, in top positions at Hewlett-Packard have had a technical background. John Young, for example, holds an electrical engineering degree, and Lew Platt a mechanical engineering degree. They also benefited from having a variety of jobs within the company, including assignments requiring a good knowledge of electronics and computer technology.

In recent years many of the young people coming into HP have had two degrees, one in engineering or science and the other an MBA. Although I'm not a strong advocate of a formal business school education, there is no question that anyone aspiring to an important management position at HP should be well grounded in all aspects of business and finance.

Chapter 12

Responsibility to Society

I HAVE STRONG recollections of the depression years in Pueblo, Colorado, in the 1930s. Although no one in our neighborhood was considered wealthy, there were poor families with virtually no income. Those who were fortunate enough to have means to support their own families shared willingly and voluntarily with those who could not provide food, clothing, or shelter for themselves. This personal experience left a lasting impression with me of the importance of personal caring and involvement.

Among the Hewlett-Packard objectives Bill Hewlett and I set down was one recognizing the company's responsibility to be a good corporate citizen.

Responsibility to the society in which a company operates is now widely recognized and accepted by American business. But it wasn't always so. I recall a conference I attended in the late 1940s that included people from various industries and organizations. We began talking about whether businesses had responsibilities beyond making a profit for their shareholders. I expressed my view that we did, that we had important responsibilities to our employees, to our customers, to our suppliers, and to the welfare of society at large. I was surprised and disappointed that most of the others disagreed with me. They felt their only responsibility was to generate profits for their shareholders.

Looking back, I suppose I shouldn't have been surprised. During the early decades of the twentieth century, profit was the businessman's sole objective. Labor was considered a commodity that could be bought and sold on the market.

Today Hewlett-Packard operates in many different communities throughout the world. We stress to our people that each of these communities must be better for our presence. This means being sensitive to the needs and interests of the community; it means applying the highest standards of honesty and integrity to all our relationships with individuals and groups; it means enhancing and protecting the physical environment and building attractive plants and offices of which the community can be proud; it means contributing talent, energy, time, and financial support to community projects.

We have a long history at HP of encouraging our people, as individuals, to participate in projects and organizations aimed at benefiting their local communities or the broader society. Bill Hewlett and I began to be involved in activities outside HP as early as 1948, when I began serving on the Palo Alto school board. Bill, in the meantime, was active in the Institute of Radio Engineers, the national society for electrical engineers, and served as its president in 1954. In this capacity Bill became acquainted with members of the IRE all across the country. Since many of these engineers were present or potential HP customers, Bill's presidency was very helpful to the company.

Service as Stanford Trustee

In 1954 I was asked to join the Stanford board of trustees. Wally Sterling had been appointed president of the university, and plans had been made to increase and strengthen the faculty and to move the medical school from San Francisco to the campus in Palo Alto. When I became a member of the board, Jim Black, a fellow trustee and the president of the Pacific Gas and Electric Company, was very helpful to me. He knew the presidents of the boards of the top private universities in the country, and through Jim I became acquainted with them.

Juan Trippe, president of Pan American Airlines, headed the board of Yale University, and Neil McElroy was president of the Harvard board. They and the board presidents of a number of the other prestigious private universities thought these schools should be considered "bell cow" universities—leaders of the pack, so to speak. I was elected president of the Stanford board in 1958, and so I was included in this group. I recall our having a meeting with Congressmen Melvin Laird and John Fogarty, of Wisconsin and Rhode Island, respectively. Their committee—the Health, Education and Welfare and Labor Subcommittee of the House Committee on Appropriations—was the congressional group that authorized overhead allowances on federal research contracts with universities. We asked the committee to authorize a 15 percent allowance for the bell cow universities, to which it agreed. I met Mel Laird only on this one occasion before he was appointed U.S. secretary of defense and became my boss at the Pentagon about ten years later.

During the mid-1960s the bell cow universities took the lead in eliminating ROTC programs from their campuses and in some cases supporting activities that I thought were not in the universities' best interest. At the Council of Foundations in New York City, I made a speech that received considerable attention. I urged increased corporate support in the form of larger contributions to universities, but suggested that these contributions be earmarked for specific uses. Many university people took exception to this but that is how I felt at the time.

During my six years on the Stanford board, the trustees and the university were faced with some major challenges and became involved in some important projects. One was the further development of portions of the Stanford lands for commercial and industrial use.

After setting aside nearly half of Stanford's 8,800 acres for future campus and academic use, university trustees and managers embarked on a program of selectively leasing portions of the remaining lands. Thus was born the highly successful Stanford Shopping Center and later, the Stanford Industrial Park, whose initial tenant was Varian Associates. The park is now home to scores of high-technology companies, including Hewlett-Packard.

As mentioned earlier, one of the major events during my term as board president was the Stanford medical school and hospital's move from San Francisco to Palo Alto, where a new medical center and hospital were built on the Stanford campus. Construction was a joint project of Stanford and the city of Palo Alto. The medical school had been in San Francisco for decades, and many of its doctors were reluctant—and some resentful—to move to Palo Alto. In the end, however, the move was made and proved to be of great benefit to the medical faculty and staff, to Stanford, and to the community. Bill Hewlett, who always has had a keen interest in medicine and education, served as president of the medical center and hospital from 1958 to 1962.

I was privileged during my tenure on the Stanford board to have former president Herbert Hoover as a friend and mentor. President Hoover was in fact a member of Stanford's first graduating class. He served as a Stanford trustee from 1912 until his death in 1964. Hoover's devotion to the welfare of mankind was a motivating factor throughout his life. His many years of public service had a great effect in contributing to a higher ethic. But he was very firm in supporting the positions he believed in.

During my term as chairman of the Stanford board of trustees, I had one particularly ticklish encounter with President Hoover. He was concerned that Wally Sterling, then president of Stanford, was going to let the faculty take over the appointment of the board of overseers of the Hoover Institution at Stanford.

President Hoover wanted his institution to demonstrate the evils of communism. The faculty maintained that the institution's research should not have its outcome determined in advance. I spent some considerable time trying to reconcile these two viewpoints. Once a month, I'd journey to New York City to breakfast with President Hoover in the sunny corner of his apartment at the Waldorf Towers. The situation was particularly difficult for me because Lucile and I were very good friends with Easton Rothwell, director of the Hoover Institution, and President Hoover wanted him replaced with Glenn Campbell, whom President Hoover had known for some time.

We finally solved the problem. The donor, President Hoover, had a right to say what he wanted his institution to do. At the same time research should be broad and objective and not subject to any preconceived outcome. Unfortunately, President Hoover was not sure the trustees would hold to that position, so he took his personal papers to his home in West Branch, Iowa.

In later years, President Hoover often invited Lucile

President Herbert Hoover with Lucile Packard, c. 1960. The photograph is inscribed "to Mrs. Packard with affection Herbert Hoover."

and me to visit him at his houseboat in Key Largo, Florida, for a week in January. This gave us an unusual opportunity to know him. We were there the week in 1961 when President John Kennedy was inaugurated. President Hoover flew up to Washington, but it was snowing, so he returned to Key Largo, where Lucile and I and the president watched the inauguration on TV.

President Hoover was an ardent fisherman. He was too old to go out fishing when we visited Key Largo, but he always had his favorite guide available to take Lucile and me out bonefishing. He would go down on the dock to see us off and be there to greet us when we returned. He had written a book called *Fishing for Fun and to Wash Your Soul*. He said in his book that "all men are created equal before fish." We spent many enjoyable evenings listening to his stories about his eventful life.

Many other HP people have served as trustees of their alma maters, including Bill Hewlett (Stanford, 1963–1974). And of course thousands more have engaged in fund-raising and other activities benefiting not only their own universities but all levels of education throughout the United States and abroad. Some of our people have taken leave from their jobs, or have been "loaned" by the company, to teach or to create special educational programs.

In their local communities, HP people often serve on planning commissions, school boards, transit districts, city councils, and other organizations charged with community responsibility. Some serve as elected officials, others volunteer their expertise. In the latter category was a team of HP engineers, headed by Vice President Barney Oliver, who in 1973 helped solve a train detection warning problem in the San Francisco Bay Area's new rapid transit system (BART). The solution devised by the HP team of volunteers, presented at no cost to BART, enabled the system to operate with full effectiveness and safety.

HP people have stood for office in local elections. In the 1950s our college classmate Ed Porter served as a Palo Alto city councilman and as mayor for five consecutive one-year terms, even becoming head of the League of California Cities—a high tribute for a mayor of a city of only about fifty thousand people.

But the involvement of HP people in their local communities is not always without surprises and difficulties. In the 1970s an embarrassing incident occurred in the HP plant community of Loveland, Colorado. In the local election, three HP employees were candidates for the city council, and all had declared their candidacy, unbeknownst to one another, on the last day they could do so. Some members of the community were not happy having three people from the same employer running for office at the same time, and one of our Loveland managers tried to persuade at least one of the candidates to drop out. He was unsuccessful, but because of the publicity, all three of the HP candidates lost. Though the incident was embarrassing, it clearly demonstrated that the involvement of an HP employee in community activities is an individual matter.

In the 1960s, as our company began to grow and expand out of Palo Alto, the potential to provide benefits to both company and community guided us in selecting sites for future plants. Through the years we have chosen sites that are close to good universities and airports, that provide a supply of skilled workers, that have strong environmental standards, and that are attractive places to live and work.

It also is important that the prospective community *want* the company rather than simply putting up with its presence. The community must be convinced that its new neighbor, in addition to providing jobs, will be a good corporate citizen and a catalyst for community betterment.

On the state, national, and international levels, Bill and I have always encouraged our people to exercise their right to vote and to speak out on issues directly affecting not only business but also society at large. I strongly believe we have a responsibility to vote no matter what our stand on candidates and issues.

Applying HP Management Policies at the Defense Department

Hewlett-Packard has sold its products to the Department of Defense (DOD) from the very early years, primarily from our commercial line of electronic measuring instruments. But we have also sold products made to military designs and specifications. I had never given a thought to any personal involvement at the DOD until I received a telephone call from Mel Laird that resulted in my serving as his deputy in 1969, 1970, and 1971. I also served on several advisory commissions in the years that followed.

The Call

In December 1968, Bill and I were hunting at our ranch in Merced when I received a call from Mel Laird, whom I had not seen since our meeting about bell cow universities in 1959. He asked me to give him some names from the business community whom he might consider for his staff at the Pentagon. He had just been designated by President-elect Richard Nixon to be the secretary of defense.

I sent him some names of people he could consider, and he called me back and asked me to meet him in Washington. So we met at the Baltimore airport early one evening. We drove to his transition headquarters at the Carlton Hotel and discussed some of the things he wanted to do when he took office. After a few hours of discussion, he said he wanted me to join him as his deputy secretary. This sounded intriguing, but the conflict-of-interest requirements were very strict. I would have to give all of the income from my HP stock and any increase in principal to charity during my term at defense. I told him I was interested in joining him and that I would let him know in a few days whether I could do so. I told him I would have to discuss his offer with my wife, Lucile, with Bill Hewlett and the directors of our company, and with several of my friends who knew something about the Defense Department.

I returned to Palo Alto and spent a week or so considering this opportunity. Lucile thought I needed a change and that I should do it. I knew that Bill Hewlett could manage the company just as well as I could and that he had a strong team of management people to support him. There were some charities that I wanted to help, and considering all aspects of the situation—including the fact that I thought it was my duty to serve my country—I decided I would join Mel Laird as his deputy secretary.

I told Mel that I would take the job and I spent most

of the time before the inauguration in January working with Mel to plan what we would do.

I knew that Robert McNamara, secretary of defense during the Kennedy and Johnson years, had alienated the professional military people in the department. There were many stories of McNamara's clashes with the brass. One of these was about the blockade to stop the buildup of Soviet missiles in Cuba, a situation that became known as the Cuban Missile Crisis.

Bob and his deputy called Admiral George Anderson, the chief of naval operations, to give him some instructions about the blockade. Admiral Anderson's reply was said to be, "You and your deputy go back to your offices. The navy is running this blockade." I think Bob McNamara was right. He should have had a say as part of the administration about how the blockade was to be handled.

Participatory Management

Mel wanted to implement a plan he called participatory management, and this fit well with the HP policies I wanted to put into effect there.

Shortly after my arrival at the Pentagon, I called on all four of the Joint Chiefs in their offices and told them I wanted to work with them and that I needed their help.

Bill and I had a deer hunt every year at our San Felipe ranch southeast of San Jose. He and I brought all the food, and we cooked and served the meals and washed the dishes ourselves with the help of our guests. In the spirit of friendship and collaboration, I invited the Joint Chiefs to join us at the deer hunt in 1969. They came and each got a deer. When it was time to wash the dishes, they rolled up their sleeves and helped us. That hunt helped establish a good rapport with the Joint Chiefs. In the following years we had a caterer to serve the food, and I continued to invite some of the Joint Chiefs to hunt with us every year I was at the Pentagon and for a number of years after I returned to HP. In fact, I got to be pretty good friends with all of them.

Dave Packard being sworn in as U.S. deputy secretary of defense in 1969. Left to right: Melvin Laird, secretary of defense, Lucile Packard, and Dave Packard.

There was an undersecretary's committee that prepared all of the documents on security matters for Nixon's cabinet. Henry Kissinger was chairman; I represented the DOD; Dick Helms, the CIA; Elliot Richardson, the State Department; Lee Dubridge and then Ed David were the president's science advisers; Jim Schlesinger represented the Bureau of the Budget; and sometimes others were involved, depending on the subject to be considered.

Our first assignment for President Nixon was to consider how much the defense budget could be reduced to provide more money for domestic programs. This was to implement the Nixon Doctrine, which was to ask the countries we were supporting to provide for their own security with help from us, to work for world peace, and to rely on negotiation rather than armed conflict.

I supported this challenging initiative because I thought it was the right way to go. But the policy could not work unless it was supported by military strength, and I felt quite sure we could provide adequate strength with a lower level of funding. I told the military chiefs that I wanted them to participate in deciding where reductions in the budget might be made. I also told them that after I made a decision I would ask each of the services involved to have a hearing before I would present the proposed reduction to the undersecretaries committee.

We had to make substantial cuts in just a few weeks, and we had very good support from the professional military people.

Procurement

One unfortunate legacy of the prior administration was the "total package procurement" plan. Under that plan contractors who wanted to bid on military weapons were required to bid for the entire job of developing, testing, and manufacturing them. This might be a good theory, but it was simply impossible to make a bid on a weapons system that had not yet been designed.

Almost all of the programs under the total package procurement policy were in trouble, and we had to figure out how to deal with them. The C5A was a large transport plane whose specifications could have been relaxed in a number of places without seriously reducing its capability. When we offered to reduce the requirements, the lawyers said we had to reduce the price because it was a valid contract. This put us in a very difficult position, and in the end I had to go back to Congress to get some more money to save these programs.

One procurement problem that came up shortly after I took office concerned supplies we bought from three southern textile mills. The previous administration left this problem for us to deal with, and they thought we would trip up on it. These mills had not met the level of minority employment they were obliged to achieve.

Fortunately, I'd had some previous experience in a related situation, when we had expended considerable effort at HP in trying to increase the opportunities for the people in East Palo Alto, a predominately black community. While we at HP were struggling with this issue, I heard of Reverend Leon Sullivan, whose Opportunities Industrial Center (OIC) had achieved positive results for minority industrial workers in Philadelphia. I asked him to come out and help me establish a similar program in East Palo Alto, and together we set up the Opportunities Industrial Center West (OICW). To make this work I invited all of the chief executive officers of the companies in the area to join us to make sure graduates from OICW would have jobs, and the project was a great success.

I decided I would do the same thing with these three southern textile mills. I personally knew two of the chief executives of these mills, and I contacted all three of them. I told them I would award the contracts to them if they promised me that they would become involved and make sure adequate progress was achieved. All three agreed to do so.

I awarded the contracts on that basis, and immediately Senator Ted Kennedy asked me to come before his subcommittee and discuss what I had done. I explained to him that I did this because I had learned from my experience in Palo Alto that it would work. I told him we needed the material and if they did not make good progress I would have other opportunities to do something about it.

In hearings of this kind, members of the Senate from the administration's party would appear to support the person at the hearing. Senator Everett Dirksen appeared at this particular hearing and supported me. I will never forget how he said in his gravelly voice about what I had done, "He is right as rain."

The Prototype Program

I began to look at military weapons acquisition systems used by other countries and some of the successful programs of the DOD. I learned that the Desault Company in France had been able to design, build, and deliver a prototype fighter aircraft to the French military for about $25 million. In the United States, the Lockheed "skunk works" run by Kelley Johnson had delivered a number of reconnaissance aircraft in a relatively short time and at a reasonable cost.

I discussed these programs with Dr. John Foster, the Pentagon's head of research and engineering; Barry Shillito, the assistant secretary of the navy; and a number of other people, and I concluded that a prototype program should be set up to produce two prototype fighter planes and a number of other items. We got mixed up a bit by describing the prototype program by the phrase "Fly before you buy," because you cannot do exactly that without stretching out the program far too long.

I wanted to build two prototype fighter planes and use the prototype system on a number of other projects. Congress wanted us to take the money for the prototype program out of the overall budget they had approved. I resisted because of the substantial cuts each service had already taken. Congress finally allowed me to handle the program the way I thought best. We gave McDonald-Douglas one contract, and they produced a prototype plane, the F16. Northrup got the other contract for a prototype plane, the F17.

The F16 has become the best air force fighter plane, and the F17—renamed the F18—has become the best navy fighter.

Reliability

Beyond our procurement difficulties, there was a serious problem with the reliability of the vacuum-tube equipment used on all of our planes. The F4, which at the time was our best fighter plane, had a mean time between failure measured in days. In Vietnam that meant an F4 could fly only a few sorties before going in for repair. This problem was solved when we used large-scale integrated circuits a few years later.

The Joint Chiefs and Unified Command

I really did not know very much about how the DOD was managed, but I soon realized that, in fact, it had been managed by a committee—the Joint Chiefs. In theory the four services acquired the weapons and trained the forces. The services then provided the weapons and forces for combat to the Specified and Unified Commands. The most important Specified Command was the Strategic Force Command under General Curtis LeMay, with its headquarters at Omaha, Nebraska, and its Nuclear Command Post in Cheyenne Mountain at Colorado Springs. Because General LeMay was a forceful leader, this command worked well.

The Unified Commands were in a bad state because each service decided where to station its weapons and forces and the Unified Commander had little to say about their placement. In addition to that, the services paid little attention to how their forces worked with the forces of the other services. The marines' radio equipment could not communicate with the navy's radio equipment. The air force had a fleet of B52 bombers stationed on Guam. When these B52s were called in to bomb in Cambodia, they did not have a secure radio channel, so the Viet Cong knew where the bombers would strike when they left Guam and these raids were essentially worthless.

I did not learn about all of these types of problems during the three years I was at the Pentagon, but I learned enough to realize that a major change had to be made. I also learned that this is what President Eisenhower meant in his farewell address when he warned of the danger of the "military-industrial complex." The military services had too much political power, and he could not make the changes necessary to reduce that power when he was in office. After leaving my post as deputy secretary, I served on several commissions for the Defense Department, most recently as chairman of the Blue Ribbon Commission on Defense Management for President Reagan. We worked closely with Senators Barry Goldwater and Don Nickels in getting the chairman of the Joint Chiefs to be the sole uniformed officer to be adviser to the president on national security issues.

It's my belief, and many military analysts have agreed with me, that our success in the Gulf War was directly attributable to the clear chain of command from President Bush to Chairman Colin Powell and, in turn, to General Norman Schwarzkopf and his subordinate commanders.

Before I went to Washington, even the people who encouraged me to go warned me that a career in business would ill prepare me for the frustrations of government bureaucracy. And they were right. At the time, I commented that working with the Washington bureaucracy was like pushing on one end of a forty-foot rope, and trying to get the other end to do what you want!

The Washington years were also hard on the family. In the first few weeks, Lucile lost sixteen pounds. As she said at the time, "Each morning when I turned on the radio, they'd be saying something terrible about you, and that spoiled breakfast. Then at noon when I'd listen again it would be worse, and that spoiled lunch. Then you'd get home, and tell me what an awful day you'd had, and that spoiled dinner. So when was I supposed to eat?"

But after a while, she just stopped listening to the radio.

By the end of 1971, after three years in Washington, I handed in my resignation and returned to California. During that time HP stock had increased in value and I estimated that I'd given away about $20 million.

I continued to serve on several defense-related groups over the years, often with good effect. In the end, I was well pleased at the success we had enjoyed in applying sound management principles at DOD. Looking back today, I feel that Mel Laird's team contributed to a positive change in U.S. military capability. But there is a definite limit to the extent that civilian criteria can be applied to the military. Military officers operate under the strictest standards of conduct. They know that choosing a military career means committing their lives to their country. They are responsible on the battlefield knowing their failure may mean not only loss of the battle, but the loss of a war or even the loss of their country. Their reward is the recognition that they performed their duty with honor. If they fail, they are relieved of their operational duties and relegated to another post.

Return to HP

When I got back to California, I resumed my position as chairman of the board at HP, and Bill Hewlett continued as chief executive, a role he had filled since I'd left for Washington. I also agreed to serve as head of President Nixon's reelection campaign in California, a task that occupied a great deal of my time for the year after my return from Washington.

Over the years Hewlett-Packard people have served not only community organizations and government bodies but also industry and professional associations. Earlier I described the creation, in 1943, of what was known as the West Coast Electronics Manufacturers Association (WCEMA). It was born largely out of frustration; West Coast firms were receiving only a small fraction of World War II contracts coming out of Washington. There were other problems to be addressed as well, and when the war ended, WCEMA continued to grow and to be an increasingly effective voice for the industry.

Bill Hewlett and I served, and since then virtually every HP officer has been involved at one time or another in the upper echelons of the group. It is now a national organization known as the AEA (American Electronics Association). The need for the AEA and similar organizations is underscored by an important characteristic of the electronics and computer industries: The industries comprise literally thousands of small businesses, most of them too small to have their voices heard or their opinions considered. They need to band together to address common problems and concerns, to develop industry views and positions on important issues, and to help shape government interaction with the industry.

Philanthropy

Good corporate citizenship includes a commitment to providing some measure of financial support to needy and deserving organizations in our society. Corporate philanthropy, although now widespread, is a relatively recent development. Before 1950 it had not been clearly established that a business corporation had the authority to make charitable gifts. About that time, however, some enlightened business leaders began to make charitable contributions to private institutions, including many universities. Such contributions were challenged in a legal action that went to the Supreme Court. In 1953 the Court ruled that for-profit corporations did indeed have the authority to make charitable gifts when the gift would advance the general interests of the corporation and its shareholders. Also, the U.S. tax laws were changed to allow the deduction of charitable contributions up to 5 percent of profit before taxes. Since then the level of corporate giving in the United States has risen dramatically and now exceeds $6 billion a year.

Julie Packard and Dave Packard in 1984 at the opening of the Monterey Bay Aquarium, one of the interests of the Packard family foundation.

Hewlett-Packard is among the most generous corporations, with grants of money and equipment in 1994 amounting to $64.4 million. Contributions are directed, for the most part, by committees of employee volunteers. Some equipment grants include a combination of products, and employee volunteers in the sales and support organizations are critical to ensuring the equipment is configured, installed, and operated properly to satisfy the needs of recipient organizations. Grants of equipment are made to fill specific, well-defined needs.

The word *philanthropy* is derived from a Greek word that means "lover of mankind." Private endeavors for the benefit of society have existed since ancient times. Unrelated to the corporate philanthropy of the Hewlett-Packard Company are the philanthropic foundation established by my late wife and me in 1964 and the William and Flora Hewlett Foundation, incorporated in 1966.

There are countless ways in which a business enterprise, as a corporate body and through the individual efforts of its people, can make important contributions to its community and to the larger society in which it operates. The betterment of our society is not a job to be left to a few; it is a responsibility to be shared by all.

Epilogue

WHEN I THINK OF the phenomenal growth of the electronics industry over the last fifty years, I realize how fortunate Bill Hewlett and I were to be in on the ground floor. But it reminds me of a story I like to tell on myself. In my sophomore year at Stanford I took a course in American history and had the opportunity to study the westward movement beginning with the early pioneers and continuing throughout the nineteenth century. I remember lamenting that I had been born one hundred years too late, that all the frontiers had been conquered, and that my generation would be deprived of the pioneering opportunities offered our forebears. But in fact, we went on to make breathtaking advances in the twentieth century.

During this century, science became the dominating factor in the progress of the world. There were two world wars that took the lives of millions of people. But at the end of the century, there is a real prospect that there will be no more world wars, although it seems that the senseless killing of people in numerous religious and ethnic groups will continue for some time.

In the twentieth century we have experienced dizzying progress, most of it founded on scientific principles established over many years in the past. This science, largely in place by the end of the nineteenth century, was based on the concept that the atom was the smallest particle in the universe and that its structure consisted of a nucleus of protons and neutrons surrounded by rings of electrons. From this concept, the periodic tables were constructed and the atom bomb developed.

At the end of World War II, we and our allies and the Soviet Union embarked on a massive program of high-energy physics in the quest to secure military advantage. Neither side ever achieved this goal, but in the process it was discovered that the atom was not the smallest particle in the universe but that the atom itself contained ten smaller particles, with weak forces and strong forces that did not obey the Newtonian laws of gravity. Using the old notion of the atom, we could simulate materials that occurred in nature such as diamonds. But with the new understanding of the atom, we can create materials that do not occur in nature— materials that are harder than diamonds, glass that is ductile. This discovery has unleashed the whole new field of genetic engineering, offering a whole new world of scientific opportunity. Everywhere I look I see the potential for growth, for discovery far greater than anything we have seen in the twentieth century.

Exponential growth is based on the principle that the

state of change is proportional to the level of effort expended. The level of effort will be far greater in the twenty-first century than it has been in the twentieth century. Hewlett-Packard Company is a good case-in-point. It took forty years for the company Bill Hewlett and I started in 1939 to reach one billion dollars in annual sales and a major part of that was from inflation. In the 1994 fiscal year that ended last October, we began the year with twenty billion dollars in worldwide sales and added five billion to that by year's end. This occurred with essentially no inflation. Other technology companies have shown similar growth.

Just as it has in the past, our growth in the future will come from new products. In 1994, we spent two billion dollars in new product development. Beginning in 1939 we generated at least six dollars of profit, spread over five or six years, for every dollar spent on new product development. By new products, I mean products that make real contributions to technology, not products that copy what someone else has done. This must be our standard in the future just as it has been in the past.

Recently there has been much discussion about developing an information superhighway. This can be accomplished with products and technology already in place. The twenty-first century, however, will be much more than an information age. It will be an age in which many kinds of new products contribute to a better life for all of the people in the world. Our company will work hard to contribute its share.

Historical Highlights of Hewlett-Packard Company

1938

• Dave and Lucile Packard moved into house at 367 Addison Avenue, Palo Alto, California; Bill Hewlett rented cottage behind the house and Bill and Dave began part-time work in the garage with $538.

1939

• Partnership formed January 1, 1939; coin toss decided company name.

1940

• Moved from garage to rented building next to Tinker Bell's Fix-it Shop at the corner of Page Mill Road and El Camino Real, Palo Alto.

• Sales: $34,000; employees: 3; products: 8.

1942

• Constructed first HP-owned building: 395 Page Mill Road, Palo Alto (Redwood Building).

1947

- Incorporated August 18.
- Sales: $679,000; employees: 111.

1951

- Sales: $5.5 million; employees: 215.

1957

- First public stock offering, November 6.
- HP corporate objectives written.
- HP began manufacturing in its first building in Stanford Industrial Park, Palo Alto.

1958

- HP's first acquisition: F. L. Moseley Company of Pasadena, California, producer of high-quality graphic recorders.
- Sales: $30 million; employees: 1,778; products: 373.

1959

- Established presence overseas with European marketing organization in Geneva, Switzerland, and first manufacturing plant outside Palo Alto in Böblingen, West Germany.

1960

- Established first U.S. manufacturing plant outside Palo Alto in Loveland, Colorado.

1961

- Entered medical field with purchase of Sanborn Company, Waltham, Massachusetts.
- Listed on New York and Pacific Stock Exchanges.

1962

• First HP listing on *Fortune* magazine's list of the largest U.S. industrial corporations: no. 460.

1963

• First joint venture (with Yokogawa Electric Works): Yoko-gawa-Hewlett-Packard, Tokyo, Japan.

1964

• Twenty-fifth anniversary year.
• Dave Packard elected chairman, Bill Hewlett elected president.

1965

• HP entered the analytical-instrumentation field with the acquisition of F&M Scientific Corporation, Avondale, Pennsylvania.
• Sales: $165 million; employees: 9,000.

1966

• HP Laboratories formed. The company's central research facility, it is one of the world's leading electronics industry research centers.

1969

• Dave Packard appointed U.S. deputy secretary of defense (served through 1971).

1970

• Sales: $365 million; employees: 16,000.

1977
• John Young named HP president (appointed CEO in 1978).

1980
• Sales: $3 billion; employees: 57,000.

1985
• HP Laboratories opened research facility in Bristol, England.
• Sales: $6.5 billion; employees: 85,000.

1987
• Bill Hewlett retired as vice chairman of the board of directors. Walter Hewlett (son of Bill) and David Woodley Packard (son of Dave) elected to the board of directors.

1988
• Surpassed $10 billion in orders for the first time.
• HP listed on Tokyo stock exchange—first listing outside the United States.
• HP moved into top 50 on *Fortune* 500 listing: no. 49.

1989
• Fiftieth anniversary year.
• HP listed on four European stock exchanges: London, Zurich, Paris, and Frankfurt.
• Acquired Apollo Computer, Chelmsford, Massachusetts, workstation manufacturer.

1990
• HP Laboratories opened research facility in Tokyo, Japan.
• Sales: $13.2 billion; employees: 91,500.

1992
- Lew Platt named HP president and CEO.

1993
- Dave Packard retired as chairman of the board of directors.
- Lew Platt named chairman, president, and chief executive officer.
- Shipped ten-millionth HP LaserJet printer.
- Sales: $20.3 billion; employees: 96,200.

1994
- Sales: $25 billion; employees: 98,400.
- Donated more than $64 million to education and other nonprofit organizations.

In 1989, the HP garage (far left) was designated a California State Historical Landmark as the birthplace of Silicon Valley. Bill Hewlett and Dave Packard at the dedication ceremony.

Product Innovation at HP

• When introduced, each of the inventions listed below represented a major advancement in state-of-the-art technology. While by no means all-inclusive, the list conveys the pace at which technology evolved and advanced in the last fifty-four years and the agility with which Hewlett-Packard Company was able to react to new technological opportunities.

1939

• Bill Hewlett's Stanford study of negative feedback resulted in HP's first product—an audio oscillator. The principle of feedback provided the foundation for other early HP products such as a harmonic wave analyzer and several distortion analyzers.

1943

• HP first entered the microwave field with signal generators developed for the Naval Research Laboratory and a radar-jamming device. A complete line of microwave test products followed World War II R&D. With many contributions in the frequency range between audio and microwave, HP became the acknowledged leader in signal generators.

1951

• The measurement of frequency was revolutionized by HP's accurate and easy-to-use high-speed frequency counter.

1960

• An HP oscilloscope was the first to use new sampling techniques to view the faster digital waveforms used in computer technology.

1963

• The commercial application of frequency synthesis resulted in the first synthesizer to generate an electrical signal at the precise frequency desired. This product, the result of a concerted team effort, provided almost unheard-of resolu-

HP's atomic clock is carried aboard a Swissair jet at Kennedy Airport in New York prior to takeoff for Switzerland to synchronize international time standards, 1964.

tion. It had an added advantage in that it was electrically programmable—an important feature in the rapidly developing world of automated testing.

1964

• HP's microwave spectrum analyzer was the first to make direct-reading, calibrated analysis of individual signals within a frequency band.

1966

• HP introduced its first computer. It was developed as a versatile instrument controller for HP's growing family of programmable test and measurement products. This combination of computer and measurement technologies gave HP a competitive edge that exists to this day.

1967

• Noninvasive fetal heart-rate monitor developed by HP GmbH in Germany helped babies by detecting fetal distress during labor.

• For a number of years HP had had an interest in the accurate measurement of frequency and time with most of the effort expended on frequency. However, the company felt it should pursue the developing field of atomic standards. In 1964 HP had developed a highly accurate portable cesium-beam standard, and by 1967 HP engineers had flown their clocks utilizing this standard to eighteen countries to synchronize international time standards. Eventually cesium-beam standards became the international standards for time.

1968

• World's first programmable scientific desktop calculator introduced by HP. The calculator, really a desktop computer, combined reverse Polish notation with a special algorithm that could handle trigonometric and logarithmic functions.

• HP introduced its first light-emitting diodes, making a significant advance in display technology.

1969

• First robotic sample injector for chromatography allowed samples to be analyzed while system was unattended.

• HP marketed its first time-shared operating system on a minicomputer supporting up to sixteen users.

1970

• A fully automated microwave network analyzer was introduced. It became an indispensable tool for the design and manufacture of microwave systems.

1971

• Work with lasers produced a laser interferometer capable of measuring to millionths of an inch. The HP laser interferometer is still the tool of choice in chip manufacturing. Similar technology produced a laser instrument that later resulted in the first electronic surveying tools.

1972

• HP took scientific calculation to the handheld level. The HP 35 handheld calculator was an instant success, making the slide rule obsolete.

1973

• HP's small, general-purpose computer system was the industry's first commercially distributed data-processing system.

• In the late 1960s the company had begun to design instruments using integrated circuits, and HP engineers soon discovered that the oscilloscope, which had been critical to analog design, was deficient for digital logic design. So HP developed logic analyzers. They became the tools of choice for engineers in the fast-growing field of digital electronics.

1974

• First minicomputer to be based on 4K dynamic random access semiconductors (DRAMs) instead of magnetic cores.

• The first HP desktop electronic calculator, introduced in 1968, was programmable, storing programs on small magnetic cards. In 1974 HP built a handheld calculator that had both programmability and magnetic card read/write capability. Integrated circuits greatly expanded the memory and hardware capabilities of the unit.

1975

• HP decided to simplify instrument systems by creating a standard interface. In 1975 the industry adopted the HP-IB interface bus as an international standard allowing one or a number of instruments to connect easily to a computer.

1976

• HP introduced a microprogrammed software package that allowed technical computer programs such as FORTRAN to run ten times faster.

1978

• HP engineers created a new computer language called ECG Criteria Language (ECL). One of the first artificial intelligence systems, it enabled HP computer systems to analyze electrocardiograms in a way similar to that of a doctor.

1979

• HP introduced fused-silica capillary columns to simplify chemical analysis and allow more compounds to be analyzed.

• A new diode-array detector for chemical analysis provided rapid results by measuring multiple wavelengths of light simultaneously.

1980

• A sixty-four-channel cardiac ultrasound product was introduced, fast enough to produce real-time, moving images of the heart beating.

• HP introduced the first laser printer fast and inexpensive enough for use outside a central computer room.

1981

• HP's NMOS-III technology produced a silicon chip with 600,000 transistors, more than any other chip on the market for many years to come.

1982

• Electronic-mail system developed by HP Ltd. in the United Kingdom was the first major wide-area commercial network of its kind based on minicomputers.

• HP's Signal Data Network was the first to relay data fast enough to allow monitoring of twenty-four hospital beds from one central station.

1984

• Thermal ink-jet technology developed at HP was introduced in a high-quality, low-price personal printer.

• HP introduced the HP LaserJet, now the world's most popular personal desktop printer.

1985

• World's first microprocessor-based network analyzer allowed users to make fast and convenient magnitude or phase-response measurements in near real time across previously unheard-of frequency ranges.

1986

• HP was the first major computer company to introduce a precision architecture based on reduced instruction set computing (RISC).

• Both Yokogawa-Hewlett-Packard and the Böblingen Instrument Division introduced semiconductor test systems that became leaders in the industry.

1988

• Digital Multimeter made high-frequency, high-accuracy, and high-resolution voltage measurements with one instrument.

• HP NewWave software environment used a graphic interface making computers easier to use, merging different types of data and automating routine tasks.

• New animation superworkstation showed motion for uses such as weather forecasting, medical imaging, and mechanical design.

• Analyzer able to measure the terahertz transmission bandwidths developed for use in optical telecommunications.

1989

• HP's new atomic-emission detector was the first analytical instrument capable of detecting all of the elements in gas chromatography except helium.

• HP introduced TMSL (Test and Measurement Systems

Language) to solve the problem of having to write software to communicate with different instruments in a test system. TMSL was opened as the basis for a new industry communications standard.

1990

• A breakthrough in semiconductor technology resulted in the CMOS chip giving high-end minicomputers the power of mainframes.

• HP entered the sample preparation field with its new supercritical fluid extractor.

1991

• The HP color scanner allowed computers to read photographs and other visual images.

• Based on ink-jet technology, HP introduced a plain-paper color printer to the home and office market.

• HP's palmtop personal computer was a breakthrough. The 640K PC weighs eleven ounces, is the size of a checkbook, and incorporates infrared wireless communication capabilities.

1992

• HP introduced a 1.3-inch disk drive. The world's smallest disk drive, the Kittyhawk personal storage module, was designed for use in very small battery-powered computing devices.

• A new cardiovascular ultrasound system produced an image of a heart, allowing doctors to perform noninvasive cardiac analysis in real time.

• The Optical Spectrum Analyzer was an important new product for use in the fast-growing optical communications field.

• HP's new modular oscilloscope was introduced, to be used in the design of high-speed, digital electronics products.

1993

• Capillary electrophoresis analytical system offered new separation capabilities for bioscientists.

• Network monitoring system introduced giving telecom providers real-time data on network problems. It also included investigation and diagnostic capabilities.

• HP introduced the smallest, lightest portable personal computer on the market. Weighing less than three pounds, it runs for eight hours on AA batteries.

1994

• HP produced the world's brightest LEDs. With bright output, reliability, and low power consumption, they replaced incandescent lamps in many new applications.

Vintage Charts

HP Products by Year of Introduction

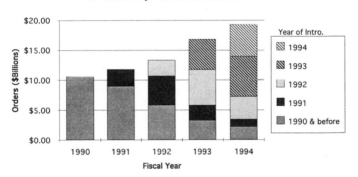

Early HP Instruments by Year of Introduction

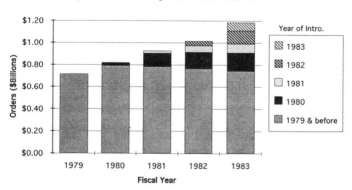

These graphs represent HP product orders by year of introduction.

Each bar indicates the year's total products orders, with

the top section of each bar showing orders for products introduced in that year.

The most recent graph illustrates the key role new products played in HP's growth in recent years.

By comparison, the earlier graph shows the longevity of HP products before the predominance of personal computers and other digital products.